Sisters of the Dark Moon

"I have always been drawn to the Dark . . . "

"It is not that I am particularly gloomy in my outlook on life, and it is not that I am fixated on the macabre, though I do enjoy scary movies and books.

"It is just that the Dark holds mystery out to me. The Dark embraces me and heals me. The sunlit spiral dances deosil in celebration of the sun, while the inward spiral of the Dark curls widdershins to explore the unknown parts of what is. It is the unraveling of self and the rediscovery of self.

"The journey of the Dark Moon explores the unknown within so that we can weave and balance the sunlit and moonlit part of ourselves."

—Gail Wood

About the Author

Gail Wood discovered the Goddess and the religion of Wicca in the mid-1980s, becoming a priestess and pursuing a "mostly" solitary practice. She teaches classes in Wicca, ritual, Tarot, and Reiki, and writes for newsletters and magazines. This book evolved from a correspondence course that she developed and has operated for three years, designed for groups interested in doing ritual and exploring the Dark Moon.

To Write to the Author

If you wish to contact the author or would like more information about this book, please write to the author in care of Llewellyn Worldwide and we will forward your request. Both the author and publisher appreciate hearing from you and learning of your enjoyment of this book and how it has helped you. Llewellyn Worldwide cannot guarantee that every letter written to the author can be answered, but all will be forwarded. Please write to:

Gail Wood
℅ Llewellyn Worldwide
P.O. Box 64383, Dept. 0-7387-0095-9
St. Paul, MN 55164-0383, U.S.A.

Please enclose a self-addressed stamped envelope for reply, or $1.00 to cover costs. If outside U.S.A., enclose international postal reply coupon.

Many of Llewellyn's authors have websites with additional information and resources. For more information, please visit our website at www.llewellyn.com.

Sisters of the Dark Moon

13 Rituals of the Dark Goddess

Gail Wood

2001
Llewellyn Worldwide
St. Paul, Minnesota 55164-0383, U.S.A.

First Edition
First Printing, 2001

Book design and editing by Connie Hill
Cover design by Gavin Duffy
Cover photo © by Photodisc Stock Imagery
Interior illustrations by Hrana Janto

Library of Congress Cataloging-in-Publication Data
Wood, Gail, 1952–
Sisters of the dark moon : 13 rituals of the dark goddess / Gail Wood
p. cm.

ISBN 0-7387-0095-9 (pbk)
1. Magic. 2. New moon—Miscellanea. 3. Goddess worship.
4. New moon—religious aspects. I. Title.
BF1623.M66 W66   2001
133.4'3—dc21   2001038068

Llewellyn Publications
A Division of Llewellyn Worldwide, Ltd.
P.O. Box 64383, Dept. 0-7387-0095-9
St. Paul, MN 55164-0383, U.S.A.
www.llewellyn.com

Printed in the United States of America

Table of Contents

Introduction

Sisters of the Dark Moon evolved from fifteen years of personal solitary practice of the religion of Wicca, the native European earth religion which includes healing, study, magic, craft, and transformation in its practices. Today a great deal of information is published about Wicca and its beliefs and practices; when I began there was very little. Even to this day, there is very little published about the Dark Moon and her energies. *Sisters of the Dark Moon* looks at the moon throughout the lunar year—thirteen moons, thirteen dark moons in which to examine the Dark Moon energy through the seasons and in each sign of the Zodiac.

Wiccans believe in the energy of the moon as she courses through the sky on her visible personal journey. She cycles from fertile and light to complete and utter darkness. We feel the tides ebb and flow even in our bodies, which are nearly all water. We feel her pull us and push us. The energy of the moon becomes our personal journey as well. So, what does it mean when we read so little about the Dark Moon? Many writers make no distinction between the New Moon and the Dark Moon, but I believe there is a great deal of difference in the energy between New Moon and Dark Moon energies. This book is an exploration of that difference and what it means to us throughout the year and through the years of our lives. This exploration will take place in ritual. Ritual is a sacred activity that connects each one of us to the Divine, to both the immanent and external Sacred.

When I began my journey into Wicca, it was like walking into a new land without a map and without direction. I began by noting the cycles of the moon and how I felt about them. The first full year, I celebrated the sun holidays and each Full Moon. I found out that the Universe is not only a safe place, but also a loving place. That was my initiation into Wicca. My celebrations were simple, unlike the rituals you will find in this book. It took me a long time to understand the nature of ritual and to have the confidence to write and do my own. I did not realize that rituals could be as simple or as elaborate as you choose. It is your own mindfulness and intent that makes a ritual sacred, not the "smells and bells" of an elaborate ritual, though those can be very effective.

It slowly became apparent to me that while I celebrated the cycles of the moon, it was the Dark Moon that had the most meaning and that embraced me unlike all the other cycles. It was then that I realized that I was on a Dark Moon Path. I then began to explore what that meant. What you will read is what the Dark Moon and the Dark Moon Path means to me. There are no secrets on the Dark Moon Path, but there are mysteries. We will explore the mystery of the Dark Moon as we learn to feel her Dark Energy and not fear the Dark.

I have always been drawn to the Dark. It is not that I am particularly gloomy in my outlook on life and it is not that I am fixated on the macabre, though I do enjoy scary movies and books. It is just that the Dark holds mystery out to me. The Dark embraces me and heals me. The sunlit spiral dances deosil in celebration of the sun, while the inward spiral of the Dark curls widdershins to explore the unknown part of what is. It is the unraveling of self and the rediscovery of self. It is dismemberment and re-memberment.

Akin to the shamanic journey to the underworld, the journey of the Dark Moon strips us of our adornments and gives us back our own self as a brilliant jewel. The journey of the Dark Moon explores the unknown part of us so that we can weave and balance the sunlit and moonlit part of ourselves. It is important to understand that we are not trying to eradicate the Dark, but to be comfortable with it and to embrace it. Dark gives definition to the light. In the Dark, we dream. It is unknown and that is what is frightening about the Dark. The Dark contains parts of us that we have not yet accepted. Properly understood, the Dark is not dangerous and we are safe in the Dark.

I can say this with confidence because I have been in the Dark. I am a forty-plus white woman who, along with my good friend Webweaver, emerged from a fundamental Christian experience that wounded us deeply. I refer to that time as being in a black hole of anger and despair. Webweaver calls it being divorced from God. The black hole statement was truer than I knew. We were in the Dark. And we healed in the Dark. I also know that Wicca and other pagan paths are not all "tra-la-la, we all love the Goddess," but a deep path that includes joy, sorrow, happiness, and travail.

The Dark Moon Path is a path with heart. It is a path for your soul, your heart, your intellect, and your body. We will sing, meditate, dance into the Dark. There we will find not only healing but joy and love. When we find things that terrify us, we will learn to understand them. Then the Dark becomes not evil, but part of our psychic gifts and ourselves.

I see the interplay of dark and light with my dogs. Bob is a golden retriever mix, a happy-go-lucky creature with a personal philosophy that I call "joie de Bobby," a play on the French expression for joy of life, *joie de vivre*. From his actions I know that Bob believes that every being is a new friend, every vehicle is a new ride, and everything else is food. Congo is a black Lab mix; she is a loving, happy dog, but she believes it is better to bark and take two hops backward until she is sure that whatever it is will not hurt her. Their reactions to Pearl, my cat, reflect this difference. Bob joyfully bounds toward Pearl, wagging his tail. I hope he has decided she is a friend and not food. Congo is much more cautious. She will spend time just sitting, waiting for Pearl to come out of her cubbyholes. Congo has not decided whether Pearl is friend or foe, and so for now Pearl is a puzzle for Congo to figure out, which she will do patiently and quietly.

Because I live on a triangle of land bordered on one side by a busy two-lane highway and because my land is unfenced, I walk the dogs on leashes. I also live far enough out in the country so that there is no ambient light from nearby towns or cities. This has given me an interesting perspective on light and dark and on the cycles of the moon. Walking two strong, active dogs on leashes through bushes and thickets has given me a different perspective from looking out of the window and saying, "Hello, moon."

When the moon is full, it illuminates the landscape so that no other light is necessary. I can see with my eyes. The Full Moon casts shadows that are, at first, startling or scary, but after I see what they are I can easily see my way through the dark. On a clear night, the moon catches and holds my eye and my attention. I have to consciously move my attention to the rest of the sky and see the stars and planets. Often, even when the night is overcast, the moon shines through. She has great power, the lady of the Full Moon, which is why she is celebrated. She is glorious.

As the moon wanes and then waxes, the light becomes dimmer. On the darkest nights, there is very little to see but the dark. The unilluminated landscape becomes so dark that I cannot see with my eyes. Cautiously I extend my other senses. My feet become my guides. I listen more carefully to hear the cracking of branches and sometimes the hooting of an owl. Often what I hear is traffic. Sometimes, the lights from a car or truck will hit my eyes just right and the light from that vehicle will fill my vision so that I cannot see at all. I cannot seem to turn away so that I am in the dark and can see. I know how a deer might feel. It is that way with the porch light too. It will catch my eye and fill my vision with light so that I cannot see. A flashlight does not help either, since my attention becomes focused on the narrow beam of light and I miss the tree branches that reach out to thwack me at face level. In the dark, it seems, it is best to go forward in the dark.

The sky on a Dark Moon night is fabulous. It is filled with stars and constellations that seem to go on forever. There is a sense that I can see all of infinity and that I am in the middle of it. In the dark, on the ground, I have to feel my way with my other senses. Once I get the sense of the dark, I can walk confidently along, seeing the outline of the dogs, hearing their activities. If a light catches my eye, I cannot see at all. During the holiday season, my neighbors put electric candles in their many windows, which looks elegant and welcoming. The light caught my eye one day as the dogs tangled themselves and their leashes around me. I whined to myself that it was too dark, and so I could not see to untangle us all from this mess. The truth was that there was too much light. Another time, Congo tangled her long leash in a thicket of small trees and branches. Since her leash was an expensive, retractable one, I didn't want to leave it out in the elements. So I had to use my fingers as eyes to untangle the mess. Once I got over the fact that I could not see because it was too dark, I really could see in the dark. I worked with the energy of the Dark and could see.

The Moon on the Dark Moon Path:
Nine Phases of the Goddess

The Dark Moon Path begins by looking at the moon in her monthly cycles. *Sisters of the Dark Moon* looks at the thirteen moons of the lunar year and examines the Dark Moon aspect of each sign of the Zodiac. The moon also changes throughout the month as she cycles through the phases of full to dark, to full again. To begin to understand the moon as a magical part of our lives, we need to look at her in each of her aspects.

There are several ways to look at the moon during the month. Many authors and practitioners of earth-based religions look at the moon as the triple aspect of the Goddess. The Crescent Moon is the Maiden, the Full Moon is the Mother, and the New or Dark Moon is the Crone. Others, including scientists and other nature observers, view the moon cycles as eight cycles, four waxing or growing phases, and four waning or declining phases. In this view, the New and Dark Moon is thought of as interchangeable.

Pagan writers and writers on astrology have taken the phases of the moon and created aspects of the moon's cycles as aspects of the Goddess. Demetra George, in *Mysteries of the Dark Moon* (HarperSan Francisco, 1992), defines the eight cycles of the moon from light to deepest dark. The *We'moon Calendar* series defines the eight cycles of the moon as going from seed to compost. In envisioning the cycles of the moon in this way, we can see the progress and change in the life of the Goddess, and by extension we can see progress and change in our lives. The moon can be a powerful guide to understanding our lives and the changes that come.

To make a distinction between the New Moon and the Dark Moon, and building on the work of others, I look at the moon in nine phases, from new to dark. In each phase, I have seen an aspect of the Goddess as cycles through the month and through her life.

The New Moon is a waxing phase, that phase of the moon where the tiniest sliver of light shines through. It is the beginning of life and the beginning of the journey. She is the Maiden, eagerly setting forth in her journey. She is full of the vitality and confidence of youth.

The Crescent Moon is a waxing phase that has more light, but not quite half of the moon's light is appearing. She is the Amazon, a little more seasoned by experience and confident that the world can be changed if she fights for it. She knows that she is strong and she believes that she is invincible.

The First Quarter Moon is a waxing phase that is half in light and half in darkness. She is the Lover, fully sexual and loving without the burdens of worry or responsibility. She is in tune with others as well as herself, and she is full of love.

The Gibbous Moon is a waxing phase that is three-quarters light and a little dark. She is the Priestess, journeying into the spiritual. She acknowledges that there are many things hidden and sacred. She is an initiate into the mysteries of the moon and of mystical womanhood.

The Full Moon is all light. She is the Mother, fertile and nurturing. The full light shines an optimism and vision of hope throughout the world. She is full of the happiness of a beautiful and productive life.

The Disseminating Moon is a waning phase that is one-fourth dark and now the dark is overtaking the light. She is the Teacher. She knows that there are lessons to be learned from lives well lived. She knows that joy is often overshadowed by grief and she knows that the bitter and the sweet go together in a combination that spices life.

The Last Quarter Moon is a waning phase that is one-half dark and where the dark is inexorably traveling into the light and into life. She is the Elder or Grandmother. She knows about death, disappointment, and lies, but she also knows about hope, birth, and truth.

The Balsamic Moon is a waning phase that is three-quarters dark. She is the Crone. She knows about hard truths, responsibility, and action. She knows about power and how to use it badly and how to use it well. Her choices define her, sadden her, and uplift her.

The Dark Moon is all dark and is the deepest dark. She is the Weaver. She knows all that the Maiden, Amazon, Lover, and Priestess know. She has experienced what the Mother, Teacher, and Elder has lived. She has taken the power of the Crone and transformed it into a magical philosophy of life that encompasses all that is in all its complexity and contradiction.

Using the moon as an analogy or model for our lives and then viewing her as a living Goddess is not a silly or weird thing to do. Neither is taking that living Goddess and making her a part of our own lives. These steps transform our lives into a magical connection between ourselves, the natural world, and the Goddess. The Goddess is inside of us as well as outside of us, but we forget that we ourselves are divine. Thinking about that connection, feeling that connection, helps us experience that connection. We then become transformed. This is not religion. This is magic.

The Lunar Year

The moon cycles from full to dark to full again every month, and the moon also progresses through a year of cycles. There are thirteen moons in our calendar, which is a solar calendar. Years such as 1999 and 2000 are based on the progress of the sun around the Earth. Within that we can celebrate the progress of the moon as she moves throughout the Zodiac.

The Zodiac that is used in the twentieth and twenty-first centuries is a solar one based on twelve signs, but other civilizations have used other ways of tracking the stars and the seasons. Some Zodiacs have been based on the moon and have contained thirteen months. Using that as a base, I have added a thirteenth sign, Arachne, to our twelve-sign Zodiac. Each month on the Dark Moon Path celebrates an aspect of the Goddess as she takes on the personality of the particular sign of the Zodiac. Through writings and ritual, we will explore how the Goddess manifests herself in that particular Dark Moon. Ritual then brings that manifestation into our own lives.

The Dark Moon in Aquarius explores the Unseen. It is the initiation, the beginning and the entering of the Dark. It is an introduction to the spirits and the Elementals. The spirit world benefits from a relationship with us, but those benefits may not be readily apparent. Aquarius is an air sign with the Maiden aspect. Air is a breath in Aquarius.

The Dark Moon in Pisces explores Time. Time is a human invention to organize the human world. Freeing ourselves of this constrictive linear view will help us explore dimensional shifts and the sensation of being inside and outside of time. Pisces is a water sign with the Maiden aspect. Water is a drop in Pisces.

The Dark Moon in Aries will explore Identity. What does it mean to say I am and who am I anyway? Aries is a fire sign with a Maiden aspect. Fire is a spark in Aries.

The Dark Moon in Taurus explores the Body. We are spiritual beings in a physical body. We will explore loving and hating our bodies, about sex, movement, and healing. Taurus is an earth sign with a Maiden aspect. Earth is soil in Taurus.

The Dark Moon in Gemini explores Knowledge. What does it mean to know? It is about academics, analysis, intuition, and "the big bag of wind." It is about "Be smart about your spirituality." Gemini is an air sign with a Mother aspect. Air is wind in Gemini.

The Dark Moon in Cancer explores Emotion. It is about balance and healing. It is about leaving shame and guilt behind to become an emotional being. It is about home. Cancer is a water sign with a Mother aspect. Water is a stream in Cancer.

The Dark Moon in Leo explores Risk. To take a chance, to dare, to fail, or to succeed. It is a way to look at fear and think about strength. Leo is a fire sign with a Mother aspect. Fire is a flame in Leo.

The Dark Moon in Virgo explores Silence. When is it right to say something, to give advice and when is it right to say nothing; to say nothing with our eyes, our bodies, and our voices. A lot is revealed in silence. Virgo is an earth sign with a Mother aspect. Earth is a mountain in Virgo.

The Dark Moon in Libra explores Descent. The classic God and goddess stories include tales of descending into the underworld, being stripped of worldly adornments, and ascending again. Libra is an air sign with a Crone aspect. Air is a storm in Libra.

The Dark Moon in Scorpio explores Intuition. Intuition is about diving deep into the psyche and surfacing again, changed. It is about what is underneath. Scorpio is a water sign with a Crone aspect. Water is a tidal wave in Scorpio.

The Dark Moon in Sagittarius explores Creativity. What does it mean to be a part of the Craft. It is more than spells. It is magic. Sagittarius is a fire sign with a Crone aspect. Fire is wildfire in Sagittarius.

The Dark Moon in Arachne is the Dark. Arachne is a spirit sign with the Weaver aspect. The spirit is weaving and interconnecting in Arachne.

The Dark Moon spirals through the lunar year, exhibiting the qualities of the Zodiac. The rituals in this book will explore all of that and weave it all together.

The Art of Ritual

I chose deliberately to center *Sisters of the Dark Moon* on ritual. I belonged to a shamanic drumming circle and we did a very powerful drumming journey to talk with Mother Earth about the water shortages in our area. One of the messages from the spirit world was that humans had forgotten how to do rituals and we need to do more rituals to heal ourselves and to heal the world. Individual rituals create ripples in the spirit world that change and affect all realities. So that if you change yourself, you change the world.

I also chose ritual because it is a dynamic way to meld all of our being together. In ritual we use our intellect, our spiritual sense, our emotion, and our bodies. The melding of mind, emotion, spirit, and body is a powerful, transformative act. Ritual calls on us to be open to change and open to the spirit.

Ritual, as practiced by pagans, neo-pagans, and Wiccans is an art. By calling it an art, we are implying a great deal of flexibility, creativity, and individuality. The rituals practiced in a sacred manner are designed to be meaningful to the individuals and groups participating in the event. When rituals become rote and unthinking, they lose their meaning to us and the rituals lose their power to affect us and our lives. They become habit.

In high school, my drama teacher talked to us about rituals. Regardless of whether we go to church or not, we perform rituals. They may be small ones or they may be grand ones. Everybody, he said, puts on the same shoe first, whether left or right. It is an unconscious ritual that has little or no meaning. If you consciously put on your left shoe first, then it becomes a ritual act. If you think of it as a sacred activity, then it becomes an effective ritual. For example, several years ago I lived in a neighborhood where it was wise to keep the doors locked all the time. Frequently when I left the apartment, I could not remember whether I had locked the deadbolt. To reassure myself I began to say emphatically, "I locked the door," every time I left the apartment. You can expand that idea a little and add a prayer for safety.

Making unconscious acts conscious is ritual. In our spiritual lives, we do this to heighten the sacredness of our actions and of our lives. You can use any level of formality that you please. I work with someone who is still a Catholic and for whom Catholicism is a living, breathing faith. The rituals have great meaning for him. For many practicing and former Catholics, rituals had no meaning and the breath of life went out of their faiths.

I have a simple approach to ritual. Once at a pagan festival, I stood in line near someone who had been interviewing what I call the BNPs—the Big Name Pagans. What she said was that people's paganism was influenced by their former religious affiliation so that someone who was Jewish did Jewish paganism, and someone who was Catholic did Catholic Wicca. What she was referring to were not the underlying philosophical beliefs but the approach to ritual and what is meaningful. I was raised Baptist and I tend to be bare-bones in my rituals. Left to myself, I do not have elaborate costumes or long poetic summonings. However ritual is done, it is powerful because it is sacred.

I practice in a pagan circle called the Web. Together our circle has created a way to do ritual that is powerful and meaningful. The rest of this section reviews that format and provides some hints to performing rituals. Since ritual is very individual, you will adapt as you need to.

The ritual is a series of concentric circles with a center in which a central working is done. The central working is some activity, usually a meditation along with raising a cone of power. As you go into the circle you bring with you the powers of this world and the spirit world to help you with the central working.

As you leave the circle, you send the powers of this world and the spirit world on their way with thanks and blessings.

Creating Sacred Space

This is the intellectual, emotional, physical, and spiritual preparation of yourself and of the space where you will do ritual. You honor you, the space, and the spirits who join you. You spend some time thinking about the ritual and what you intend to accomplish, what you already know and what you hope to gain. You center your mind and heart on the ritual. You also prepare the physical space where the ritual is to be done. You may clean it and then do some purification such as smudging, spreading salt, sage, or a lemon juice and water combination. You may also set up an altar with candles, symbols of the ritual to be performed, and symbols of the directions and the deities. This is to disrupt the negative energy of the space and make way for a sacred ritual. You may also prepare yourself. Some people take a ritual purifying bath, others don special clothing, and others begin by toning a single note such as OMMMMMM.

Casting the Circle

Casting a circle is the physical act of separating the space in which you are working from the everyday world and moving into the space between the physical world and the spiritual world, called "being between the worlds." You can cast a circle in several ways: by visualizing a clear light of any color in a circle around you; by walking around the room with a broom, staff, rattle, or athame a symbolic number of times, usually three; by toning "A circle is cast, a circle is cast, a circle is cast," a symbolic number of times; you can put down a physical circle made of yarn, cornmeal, or salt. It is a conscious act that moves you into the realm of the sacred.

Summon the Guardians and
Elementals of the Directions

East, West, North, South, Above, and Below are the directions commonly summoned. Where you begin depends on the work you are doing and on the time of day. There are correspondences for each of the directions and I encourage you to develop correspondences such as colors, symbols, animals, and other things that are personally meaningful to you. The Guardians are the beings on the astral or spirit plane that assist you in your workings. Summoning both the Guardians and the Elementals means that you intend to change yourself in both the physical and spiritual plane. The Elementals are the beings in this physical world associated with those directions: Sylphs for the East, Salamanders for the South, Undines for the West, and Gnomes for the North. Some common correspondences for the East are air, dawn, light blue, birds, and the Tarot suit of Swords. Some common correspondences for the South are fire, noon, red, yellow, orange, and the Tarot suit of Wands. Some of the common correspondences for the West are water, sunset, blue, green, fishes, and the Tarot suit of Cups. Some of the common correspondences for the North are earth, midnight, black, brown, rocks, and the Tarot suit of the Earth, or Pentacles.

Evoke the Goddess and Evoke the God

Evoking means that you are inviting the God and the Goddess into your circle to assist you with your ritual and to help you accomplish the change you are hoping for. If you invoke the deities, you bring their presence in you. Some traditions invoke or evoke only the Goddess. The rituals in this book are designed to be flexible so I invite you to adapt them to your needs and preferences. It is important to know the deities that you are working with. If you are doing a ritual on love, it is more appropriate to invite Aphrodite than to invite the Mother-Destroyer goddess, Kali. If you have no names for the Divine presence in your life, invite them by an aspect of their personality such as Mother, Amazon, Maiden, or Crone for the Goddess and Lover, Protector, Father, or Sage for the God.

Center and Ground

Centering means that you find the center of yourself and move calmly into a peaceful state where you slough off the everyday cares and woes, moving into a sacred state where your mind, body, and spirit are connected. You can do this by breathing deeply, with a breath coming out in a single tone, such as OMMMMM. Grounding connects you with the earth and with the greater universe. This is a grounding meditation:

○ℛ Meditation

Center yourself by breathing deeply three times. With
the first two breaths exhale noisily as you shake off
the everyday world. The third breath comes out as
OMMMMMMM. Stand lightly and wiggle your feet
and toes. See tree roots growing out of your heels and
toes, and see those roots go deeply through the floor into
the ground below. See the roots go deep into the earth,
through rocks and soil, until the roots come to an anchor-
ing place. Tie your root around there as you anchor your-
self into the Mother Earth. See the roots of your toes
extend outward, not far underground, providing you with
a steadiness in the world. Feel the sap rise into your
trunk, filling your legs, torso, and head with the nurturing
power of the Earth. Lift up your arms and feel branches
extend from your fingers, going outward toward the sky.
See in your branches your past, your present, and your
future. See the scars and see the new growth. Feel the sap
energy move through your neck into your head. From
your crown, this energy bursts forth. As it moves into
the Universe, another light from far out in the Universe

*comes to meet you. See that energy move together. You
are connected to All that is.*

Statement of Ritual Intent
This is the beginning of the work you intend to do. It is a time to
state consciously what you intend to do and what you intend to
accomplish.

The Work
This is the vehicle that moves your intention into reality. It can
be a meditation, song, dance, shamanic journey, or prayers.

Raise the Cone of Power
This is the point where the work you did becomes manifest. The
cone of power gets raised, and when it is ready, the cone blasts off
into the universe. The cone of power is achieved by singing or
chanting, growing louder and faster, and then combined with
movement, also growing faster. You then send the energy with
your intention out into the Universe.

Cakes and Ale
This is a time to pause and reflect and to give thanks. You can
write down what you have learned or experienced. It is important to eat and drink something because the food and drink
grounds you, and that grounding makes the spiritual work you
have done a physical reality. The food does not have to be cakes
and ale, but should be some kind of food and drink that grounds
you.

Center and Ground
Center yourself again in preparation to leave the circle and re-
enter your everyday life. In grounding, gently pull your energy
back into yourself, both from your crown and from the roots at
your feet. Keep what energy you need and ground the rest into
the earth.

Dismiss the Guardians and Elementals of the Directions

Thank the Guardians and Elementals for their attendance and assistance in your ritual. A note about Elementals: some traditions say, "Go if you must, stay if you will," to the Elementals. That is not recommended for the Elementals who are essentially amoral and do not have all the constraints that humans do. For example, an Undine, the water Elemental, may find it extremely interesting to see a waterspout. Unfortunately for you, the Undine chose to make your hot water heater a waterspout. For you, it is an expensive disaster and for the Undine, it is interesting and probably a lot of fun. So, I recommend bidding them a firm and thankful goodbye.

Open the Circle

Whatever you did at the beginning, now perform that action backward. You are thus moving your circle back into the physical world.

How to Use this Book

I always recommend "being smart" about your spiritual life; that is one of the overall goals of this book. The more you know about yourself, about the Goddess and about the moon, the smarter you will be and the better your spiritual life will be. Questing and questioning are part of our spiritual natures. Nothing should be accepted without examining it, questioning it, dismembering it, remembering it, understanding it, experiencing it, wondering about it—and laughing at it, laughing about it, or laughing with it. Questions and laughter are needed to stay vital and alive.

There is a section for each sign of the Zodiac and each section contains a ritual. Feel free to change, reject, accept, and adapt the rituals. If it does not suit you, do not do it. Use your own knowledge and creativity to commemorate your walk in the Dark.

Spend some time getting to know the moon throughout the year and in her monthly cycle. Be aware when the moon is full or new or dark. I highly recommend a moon journal. Note how the moon travels through the month and how you feel. When is your menstrual cycle, if you menstruate? Many traditions, including native cultures, named each moon month, such as Corn Moon, Frost Moon, and Moon of the Strawberries. You may want to name the moons in a way that reflects your own inner landscape.

Do feel free to change things during your own rituals. It is important that the symbols, evocations, and poems mean something to you. In some of the rituals I leave it to you to devise your own ways of interacting with the spirit world. In all cases, it should mean something to you. It should be rich, personal, and sacred.

This book begins with the astrological sign of Aquarius. Normally the astrological year begins with Aries, but I felt that the vitality and youth of Aquarius was indicative of a Maiden aspect and I wanted to begin with a Maiden aspect. You can envision the astrological year as a large circle without beginning and end, as well. Often, we develop systems to explain our lives and then harden ourselves into thinking "this is the right way." Beginning with Aquarius in this book will help move us out of a rut and encourage us to look at things in a new way.

Don't expect this to be deadly serious all the time. I am a Sagittarius, and humor is what Sags are. This is a lunatic journey and laughter is important. Dark times often create dark humor. All of us are given to laughter to save us, to lighten our load, and to help us through the dark times. Laughter is the remembrance of joy.

You Are the Moon: A Ritual introduction to the Moon in All Her Phases

A few years ago, Webweaver and I were working with the *Medicine Cards* by Jamie Sams (New York: St. Martin's Press, 1999) and we drew the Wolf card. The last page of the explanation says, "To live is to grow, and growing comes through accepting all life forms as your teachers. Become Wolf, and take up the sense of adventure. You may just stop howling and learn to become the moon." We took it a step further to say "you are the moon." As we have read Tarot over the years, the meaning of the Moon card has taken on a deeper, richer meaning as we try to be the moon. Even now, I am not sure I know what it means to say, "I am the moon." I accept it as a mystery that I know in my being but cannot explain. In reading Tarot, I now interpret the Moon card to be that all-encompassing power that is beyond duality. It contains everything, including the contradictory energies we see as good and evil. It is a reflection of power used in its most loving way to contain all that is.

After spending years observing the moon and seeing her change in all her phases, I thought I knew the moon. Being the moon is a mystery and it will be the first mystery that we will explore in this Dark Moon journey. In exploring mysteries, we are not seeking the answer, but exploring what it is to know and to be. It is the journey, not the destination, that is important.

This ritual is designed to help you understand the cycles of the moon. I have used my nine cycles of the moon in the meditation and you will go through each cycle of the moon. You might feel that is too much for one meditation, so the meditation can be adapted so that you do one cycle at a time. If you feel drawn toward another way of looking at the moon, please use that. The point is to be the moon. You do not have to be my idea of the moon.

The meditation is in italics. I have not inserted pauses or any other kind of stage direction, so that you do not rush through it all. Take long pauses to experience the world you find in the meditation. You may want to record the meditation and then play it back during the ritual. I know for a fact that the Goddess does honor technology! And I wish you a good journey.

ℂℛ You Are the Moon
A Dark Moon Ritual

Creating Sacred Space: Think about the moon and what you know intellectually about her phases and her life during each month. Think about what you associate with the moon and how you feel about the moon. Is there a particular phase that means more to you than others? What emotions are stirred during different phases of the moon?

Cast the Circle: Walk three times clockwise around your circle, using a broom or athame to cast the circle.

> The circle is cast and I am between the worlds.
> Blessed be.

Summon the Directions. First summon the East:

> Guardians of the East and air, keepers of the mind
> and intellect, join me in my rite. Sylphs of the wind
> and breezes, bring the fresh air of a clear mind to my
> rite. Welcome Guardians and Elementals.

Summon the South:

> Guardians of the South, keepers of passion and fire,
> join me in my rite. Salamanders of the fires and
> volcanoes, bring the fiery wisdom of spiritual seeking
> to my rite. Welcome Guardians and Elementals.

Summon the West:

> Guardians of the West, keepers of emotion, join
> me in my rite, Undines of the watery depths, bring
> emotional clarity to my rite. Welcome Guardians and
> Elementals.

Summon the North:

> Guardians of the North, keepers of silence, join me
> in my rite. Gnomes of the earth and the caves, bring

the depth of silence to my rite. Welcome Guardians
and Elementals.

Evoke the Goddess:

Hecate, triple goddess, guardian of the crossroads,
join me as I become the moon. As Mother, Maiden,
and Crone, you know the phases of woman and of
the moon. Join me and guide me through this ritual
journey. Welcome.

Evoke the God:

Dionysus, god who dies and is reborn, lord of the
vine, join my rite. As he whose life follows the life-
death-rebirth of the seasons, you know the phases of
man. Join me in my rite. Welcome.

Center and Ground: See yourself standing on a dark plain
with no moon above you. Lift up your arms to embrace the Dark.
Send your roots outward from your toes and heels. From the soles
of your feet, send roots downward, deep into the ground. Anchor
yourself deep in the bosom of the Mother. Draw up power into
your body and up through your torso. Feel the power come out
through the crown of your head. Feel the Universe reach down
with its power and connect and embrace the power coming from
you. Meld together, rooted in the power of the Mother and connected to the power of the whole Universe.

Statement of Ritual Intent:

As I begin the study of the moon, I need to understand her in all her phases. I need to understand what
the phases mean the most to me and what phases
hold the most love, the most terror. I am the moon.

℞ Meditation

*Make yourself comfortable and breathe three times to
center your breathing. You find yourself in the dark, far
away from human habitations and light. Notice how you
feel and gradually you will notice that you are not afraid.
Notice your surroundings and yourself. What does your
body feel like and who are you? Appearing before you
is Wolf, your guide for this journey. Wolf will take you
through the phases of the moon. You notice a tiny sliver
of light begin to appear and it is the New Moon. See the
moon before you. Feel and see yourself going toward the
moon at the same time that the moon comes toward you.
You and the New Moon meet and join together. You are
the New Moon. Take some time to feel what that is like.
Be the New Moon. When the time is right, Wolf will
guide you to the waxing Crescent Moon. You see the
moon come toward you. You meet and join together. You
are the Crescent Moon. Be the Crescent Moon. When
the time is right, Wolf will guide you to the First Quarter
Moon. You see the moon come toward you. You meet
and join together. Be the First Quarter Moon. When the
time is right, Wolf will guide you to the Gibbous Moon.
You see the Gibbous Moon come toward you. You meet
and join together. Be the Gibbous Moon. When the time
is right, Wolf will guide you to the Full Moon. You see
the moon come toward you. You and the moon meet and
join together. Be the Full Moon. When the time is right,
Wolf will guide you to the waning Disseminating Moon.
You see the moon come toward you. You and the Moon
meet and join. Be the Disseminating Moon. When the
time is right, Wolf will guide you to the Last Quarter
Moon. You see the moon move toward you. You and
the moon meet and join together. Be the Last Quarter*

*Moon. When the time is right, Wolf will guide you to
the Balsamic Moon. You see the moon come toward you.
You meet and join together. Be the Balsamic Moon.
When the time is right, Wolf will guide you to the Dark
Moon. You see the moon come toward you. You and the
moon meet and join. Be the Dark Moon. When all is
done, Wolf will call you back to yourself. See the cycles
of the moon before you and say goodbye to them individu-
ally, and thank them for their wisdom. You have a gift for
the moon. Give it to her and ask if there are any final
words for you. Say your farewells. Wolf will guide you
back. Eventually the darkened landscape becomes day.
Wolf nuzzles your hand, leaves a gift, and with that says
good-bye for now. Take three breaths, open your eyes.
You are back in your sacred circle.*

Raising a cone of power: Take a minute to reflect on what
you've learned and what was significant. Reflect on the aspect of
the moon that was important to you. Then stand up and move,
saying or singing or chanting,

I am the Moon, I am She.
I am New, I am Crescent,
I am First Quarter, I am Last,
I am Gibbous, I am Full.
I am Disseminating. I am Balsamic.
I am the Deep Dark Moon.
I am Moon I am Moon I am Moon,
MOON,
MOON,
MOON,
MOOOOOONNNNNNN!!!!!!

(Get louder and faster until you feel the whoosh of power into
the Universe.)

Cakes and Ale: Say a prayer of thanksgiving to the moon and to the Guardians, Elementals, and the Deities. Take some time to eat and drink something as you ground your spiritual experience into this reality.

Center and Ground: See yourself back on the darkened plain, rooted in the earth and embracing the dark sky. Gently, ever so gently, disconnect your root from its anchor, knowing full well that you always have access to the groundedness and love of the Mother. Pull your roots back into your feet until you are fully back in the here and now. Turn your awareness toward your arms and head, and gently disconnect yourself from the embrace of the Universe, knowing full well that you always have the love of the Universe surrounding you. You are back, full into the circle. Blessed be.

Dismiss the Guardians and the Elementals. First dismiss the North:

> Guardians and Elementals of the Silence and the
> Dark Earth, thank you for your wisdom and power in
> my circle. Go with my thanks and my blessings. Hail
> and farewell.

Dismiss the West:

> Guardians and Elementals of the Emotional Depths
> and of the Water, thank you for your emotional
> clarity and deep heart. Go with my thanks and my
> blessings. Hail and farewell.

Dismiss the South:

> Guardians and Elementals of the Fire and of the
> noonday sun, thank you for the will to change. Go
> with my thanks and my blessings. Hail and farewell.

Dismiss the East:

> Guardians and Elementals of the Air and of clear thinking. Thank you for your wisdom and power. Go with my thanks and my blessing. Hail and farewell.

Dismiss the Goddess:

> Hecate, Goddess of the phases of woman, thank you for the wisdom you brought to my sacred rite. Go with my thanks and my blessings. Hail and farewell.

Dismiss the God:

> Dionysus, God of the phases of man, thank you for the wisdom you brought to my circle. Go with my thanks and my blessings. Hail and farewell.

Opening the Circle: Moving widdershins with the object with which you opened the circle; move three times around, chanting: "The circle is open but unbroken."

❧

The Dark Maiden

The Dark Maiden

The first steps on the Dark Moon Path begin with the Goddess as Maiden. Aquarius, Pisces, Aries, and Taurus are all maiden phases in the Dark Moon lunar year. In each of their elements, these signs are in the beginning phases of their growth so that Aquarius is a breath of air, Pisces is a drop of water, Aries is a spark of fire, and Taurus is the soil of earth. Each of these is the basic building block for their respective element. Breath becomes wind, a drop becomes a stream, a spark becomes a flame, and soil becomes a mountain. The Goddess as Maiden is also the beginning phase and we will explore her personality fully as we see the maiden in the element of air, water, earth, and fire.

Pagans have looked at the Goddess as a maiden and associated her with the Moon. The maiden, or virgin, aspect of the moon is an aspect of the goddess as "entire unto herself." She is her own creature. No one owns her. Unlike the twentieth-century definition of virgin, she may or may not be sexual. In either case, she answers to no one but herself. Her behavior is wholeheartedly dedicated and directed to what interests her. Those interests may be altruistic or they may be self-centered. The Maiden is completely committed to herself and her ideals. She is her own companion in the world.

Until I understood it this way, I was always perplexed by the stories of the Greek goddess Artemis and her Roman counterpart, Diana. She is the huntress and a virgin goddess, yet at the same time there are stories about her sexual relationships. The key is how she views and values those relationships. Even though she is sexual, her guiding purpose is not the relationship but her inner ideals. Consequently, Artemis remains the huntress, and her sexual relationships are secondary. She never changes her relational status to someone's lover or someone's mother. She is always the huntress.

We can look at Aphrodite, the Greek goddess of love in the same way. Of course, Aphrodite is a goddess who is very sexual. She has a great many relationships, including motherhood and wifehood. Yet, she remains completely committed to her work as the goddess of love. She would never be defined as Eros' mother.

So the Maiden is independent, strong, accomplished, and dedicated. The Dark Maiden aspect is all these things. The Dark Maiden knows that life and love has its dark side and that to be independent, you may be alone. She knows that to be alone is to exclude oneself from not only the cares and woes of being with others but that it also deprives her of the solace of another's consoling embrace. It is not possessing so-called bad qualities that make the Dark Maiden dark, but the knowing. The Dark Maiden knows about the dark, about so-called bad qualities, and she knows that presumed good qualities misapplied or taken to excess can do harm to herself and to others. The other truth the Dark Maiden knows is that others do exist and that her actions, independent as she is, can help or hurt others.

CR

Dark Moon in Aquarius

The Dark Moon Path begins its inward spiral as the Dark Moon moves into Aquarius, an air sign. Aquarius is a breath, which breezes into a wind in Gemini and a storm in Libra.

The story of Aquarius begins on Mount Olympus. Zeus, the father of the gods, falls in love with the Trojan youth, Ganymede. Ganymede is a youth of incredible beauty, more handsome than any other mortal, male or female. Zeus transforms himself into an eagle and swoops down and kidnaps Ganymede. Zeus carries the youth to Mount Olympus where Ganymede becomes a cupbearer to the gods. To appease the youth's family, Zeus gives them great riches and a promise. When the mortal Ganymede dies, Zeus places him in the stars as the constellation Aquarius. Ganymede shines forever in beauty and the love of Zeus. A cynical thought does creep in because Zeus' young male lover fares much better than the women Zeus variously loves, kidnaps, and impregnates.

The air sign of Aquarius is concerned with mental and social development. Aquarians are progressive, altruistic, tolerant, and inventive, committed to change, often at any cost. Turned inward, Aquarius can be disorganized, cranky, rebellious without a cause, fanatical, tearing down without building up, detached, aloof, and unthinking. Turned inward, Aquarius is unprincipled, erratic, and unfair.

In esoteric terms, the element of air concerns itself with the mind and the rational self. Air is about understanding and the ability to think and to plan. Air moves humans from the imperatives of physical need to the realm of ideas and thought. The intellect excites air signs, and the life of the mind, engaged in study and reflection, is an exceptionally exciting one for air signs.

The Air Maiden shows herself as an altruistic idealist, dedicated to her causes whatever they may be. She lives the life of the mind and the intellect. If she has not combined her intellect with the understanding of the life of the spirit, she can be dispassionate, dismissive of the feelings of others, and unthinkingly cruel. A woman of intelligence and intellect, she may be unable to tolerate people who are less intelligent or less idealistic than she. If the Air Maiden is hard on others, she is even harder on herself. She turns the critical power of her intellect inward onto herself and criticizes herself with unimaginable cruelty. She needs to learn compassion in order to become fully herself. Frederich Nietzsche said, "Whoever fights monsters should see to it that in the process he does not become a monster. And when you look long into an abyss, the abyss also looks into you" (*Complete Works*, Stanford, 1999). She looks into the abyss of the soul and sees the Dark.

During the time when the sun is in Aquarius, pagans celebrate the holiday of Imbolc, a celebration of the triple goddess Brigid, the fire goddess and guardian of the well. She rules over creativity, dedications, initiations, and the consecration of new tools. Imbolc is a holiday that celebrates new beginnings, the time when things begin to grow. The spark of creativity happens and life begins to take shape. I always envision Imbolc as the seedling nestled beneath the ground in the warm heart of the earth mother, just beginning to germinate. The seedling is putting forth its new shoots, beginning to push its way to the surface and to the sun. It is a hopeful, happy holiday.

The dark side of Imbolc is inertia. In the bleak winter landscape where I live in upstate New York, it is hard to imagine new growth and green seedlings at the beginning of February. Even if the temperatures are warm, there is ice, flooding, and the general havoc of rough weather. It makes a person want to curl up in a ball and not move.

The opposite of hope is despair. The opposite of growth is not death, but inertia or depression. Depression is not the negative feeling of being "bummed" if the car does not start or your hair looks bad, but deep dark paralysis of the whole being. You can't move, you can't think, you can't cry, and you can't laugh. You are paralyzed and numb.

This numbness influences our behavior and we may lose interest in the things that give us joy. We lose our appetite for good things such as food, sex, and pleasure. We are unable to experience pleasure or reward. There is no quality to life.

Depression is an unseen disorder and many people suffer from it in varying degrees of severity. As we move through Aquarius on the Dark Moon Path, we explore the unseen. We look into the abyss of ourselves to see what is there and this is very scary. As we deepen our spiritual work, we find that there are spirits and beings around us, willing and wanting to help us. Unseen, they help us manage our world. As our awareness increases, our awareness of the unseen increases. We see more clearly and with more compassion. I have learned to look at faults and strengths as two sides of the same coin. A strength taken to an extreme is a fault. By shifting our vision slightly we can reframe a fault into a positive characteristic, which, with work, can be a real strength.

Bravely, we move to the abyss and look into ourselves. We look clearly with our minds and we look compassionately with our hearts. With that process we transform the Air Maiden of Aquarius into an emotional adult committed to social change and intellectual challenges.

℞ Looking into the Abyss
A Ritual for the Dark Moon in Aquarius

Creating Sacred Space: Spend some time thinking about yourself and your inner landscape. Take a hard look and then add some compassion. How does compassion differ from rationalization? Begin with the room as dark as possible (use common sense and keep a light so you can see to do the activities of the ritual).

Cast the Circle: Make a circle that you can see, using yarn or thick thread. Do this in complete silence, ending with a deep breath and "I am between the worlds, blessed be."

Summon the Guardians and Elementals:

Summon the East:

> Guardians of the East, lovers of the mind and of
> learning, join me in my rite; Sylphs of the East, the
> breath of inspiration, join me in my rite. Welcome
> Air Guardians and Sylphs to my circle.

Summon the South:

> Guardians of the South, lovers of passion and will,
> join me in my rite; Salamanders of the South, the

fiery spark of resilience, join me in my rite. Welcome
Fire Guardians and Salamanders.

Summon the West:

Guardians of the West, lovers of emotion and
compassion, join me in my rite. Undines of the West,
the drop of love, join me in my rite. Welcome Water
Guardians and Undines.

Summon the North:

Guardians of the North, lovers of silence and respect,
join me in my rite. Gnomes of the North, the soil of
new growth, join me in my rite. Welcome Guardians
and Gnomes of the North. Hail and welcome
Guardians and Elementals.

Evoke the Goddess:

Hail! Brigid, Goddess of the Sacred Well, Guardian
of the Forge, join me in my rite and bring the
excitement of new beginnings. Hail and welcome
and blessed be.

Evoke the God:

Hail Green Man, god of the vegetation, he who
comes to us in the spring. Though I do not yet see
you, welcome and blessed be.

Center and Ground: You are standing on the edge of the forest. Note that your trunk, arms, and legs are that of a tree. Send
your roots downward into the earth, deep into the warm bosom
of the Mother Earth. Find a rock and anchor your root there, safe
and secure in the Mother. Raise your arms to reach the sky. See
the branches stretch far out into the sky. Feel the embrace of the
sky reach down and welcome you. Come back to yourself,
grounded in the Earth and embraced by the sun.

Statement of Ritual Intent:

Looking into the abyss of myself is a frightening act and I could see monsters. I am surrounded by the unseen world who will guide me, protect me, and comfort me. I am going to ask for their wisdom.

ℛ Meditation

You are standing on a very dark plain. You cannot see with your eyes so you extend your senses. Notice what you "see" with your other senses. The sky suddenly becomes illuminated with moonlight and you are standing on the edge of an abyss so large and so dark that you have no perception of the beginning or end of it. It is scary but know that the creatures of all the directions are there to catch you if you fall. Stand there and learn what the abyss has inside it. You do notice that the abyss is looking into you as well. Ask what the abyss sees, no matter how "good" or "bad." In a passionless, nonjudgmental way, the abyss tells you what it sees. Because there is no judgment, there is no sting and you receive the information. Thank the abyss for the information. You notice that there are other beings around you. The Guardians of the East come to you with the Sylphs. Note what they look like and how they appear to you. Ask them for words of wisdom. Listen. When they are finished, they will stand back and the Guardians of the South will come to you with the Salamanders. Ask them for words of wisdom. Listen. When they are finished, they will stand back and the Guardians of the West with the Undines will come to you. Ask them for words of wisdom. Listen. When they are finished, they will stand back and the Guardians of the North with the Gnomes will come to you. Ask them for words of wisdom. Listen. Finally, all the Guardians

and Elementals will stand around you in a comforting
embrace. Say thanks and ask for any final words of
wisdom or comfort. Suddenly they are gone in a sparkling
swirl of confetti, like dots of colors, bright, brilliant, and
sparkling. You say final thanks to the abyss and walk
away into the light. And as the light grows, you open
your eyes and you are back in the room and back in your
sacred circle.

Raising the Cone of Power: Chant or say this wish:

May the Great Ones of this world and the other
Cleanse and strengthen my mind,
May they tune my heart in accord with theirs,
May their power and love manifest in my life,
May they surround me with inspiration and grace,
Shield me from pettiness, including my own
Because I am worthy of their love.
Love, love. Love, love, love, love, love, love,
LOVE, LOVE, LOVE.
Whoosh!!!!!!!

Cakes and Ale: This is a celebration and a thanksgiving. Say a
prayer and eat a little something.

Center and Ground: Gently remove your embrace from the
sun, taking the energy of the Universe with you. Feel your roots
deep in the ground. Gently detach yourself from the anchor and
pull the root back. Keep what energy you need. Remember that
you are always connected to the love of the Universe.

Farewell to the God:

Thank you Green Man, God of the Forest, the
Vine, and the Leaf. Thank you for your wisdom that
everything dies and everything is born. Go with my
thanks and my blessings. Hail and well met.

Farewell to the Goddess:

> Thank you, bright Brigid, Lady of the Well and the Forge. Thank you for the wisdom of the fire that refines and creates. Go with my thanks and my blessings. Hail and well met.

Farewell to the Guardians and the Elementals:

Dismiss the North:

> Guardians of the North of the Great Silence, thank you for your presence in my rite. Go with my thanks and my blessings. Gnomes of Dark Mountains, thank you for the wisdom of connection. Go with my thanks and my blessings. Guardians and Elementals, hail and well met.

Dismiss the West:

> Guardians of the West of deep emotion, thank you for your feeling and your presence in my rite. Undines of the watery deep, thank you for the beauty of the sea. Guardians and Elementals, go with my thanks and my blessings. Hail and well met.

Dismiss the South:

> Guardians of the South, thank you for your passion and will. Salamanders, thank you for the fire of creativity. Guardians and Salamanders, go with my thanks and my blessings. Hail and well met.

Dismiss the East:

> Guardians of the East, thank you for your intellect and clarity. Sylphs of the feathery light touch, thank you for the refreshing breezes. Go with my thanks and my blessings. Hail and well met.

Open the Circle: Going widdershins, take up your physical circle and the circle in your mind and your spirit. When you are finished, take three deep breaths and say, "Blessed be."

Dark Moon in Pisces

We swim inward on the Dark Moon Path into the sign of Pisces, a water sign. Pisces is the drop that becomes a stream in Cancer and a tidal wave in Scorpio. Pisces is the Water Maiden.

Pisces is drawn as two fish swimming together in a circle. In Greek myth, the larger fish is Aphrodite, the goddess of love, and the smaller fish is her mortal lover, Adonis, who was killed by a boar. Together they symbolized the great yearly cycle of life from seed to fertility to harvest to death and rebirth. Aphrodite symbolized the immortal, undying, changing moon, while Adonis symbolized the mortal cycle of life, death, and rebirth.

Many ancient cultures revered the dolphin as a symbol of the fish constellation; that reverence continues in the modern-day fascination with and love of dolphins as companions to humans. In Homer's "Hymn to Dionysus" some pirates mistake the god Dionysus for a rich young prince and capture him, intending to hold him for ransom. The young god breaks free of his bonds and turns the ship's masts into grape leaves. He throws the pirates overboard and turns them into dolphins. Legends among sailors say that the dolphins remember their lives as humans and gather around fishing boats and help by guiding fish into the nets.

Pisces is a healing sign that works from the heart of compassion that is both empathetic and otherworldly. Turned inward Pisces is emotionally chaotic, moodily martyred, and confused.

In esoteric terms, the element of water symbolizes emotions. Our emotions can be a stream, an ocean, a trickle, a waterfall, the rapids, or a droplet. Water can clean us, wash over us, drown us, buoy us up, and quench our thirst. The water signs, associated with healing and emotion, are really water! By that I mean that the water signs do a thorough job of working through emotions. All three signs go through the spectrum of emotions. Pisces can be a joyous place where dreams are dreamed and the world seems to flow boundlessly into the infinite, transcending all sorrow and pain. She can become martyred and constantly complaining about her terrible lot in life.

The Water Maiden taps into the emotional flow of the Universe. She is feeling and she lives the life of the heart. When life is going well and it all works, she is happy, boundlessly compassionate, and connected to all that is. When she loses the rhythm and the step, she becomes confused and seems to drift from relationship to relationship and from feeling to feeling. A year or so ago, someone said to me that they felt that there was so much sorrow that Pisces could not possibly be a Maiden but must be a Crone. I've learned that the Maiden does feel intense sorrow like the singer in the folksong *Maid of Constant Sorrow*, who sings

"I've seen trouble all my days / and to this earth in grief and sorrow / I am bound until I die." Unlike the Crone who has been seasoned with years of living, the Water Maiden suffers sorrow with added pain because her life stretches before her endlessly and all she sees is pain. The Dark Maiden of Water can feel bound in time and space and imprisoned by emotions.

The Water Maiden needs the perspective of time to move her into a full vision of her self. Flow moves her into that sense of things moving together into a harmonious whole. When we are in flow, everything goes right and moves right along. We are engaged bodily, mentally, emotionally, and spiritually. You may feel it while doing any activity where you are completely engaged. You do not even have to be very good at it.

Several years ago, I was swimming a great deal. My body was getting stronger and slimmer and my general health and well-being improved as I swam regularly. Sometimes it was very hard to get up, get to the pool, and do all those laps. Sometimes it was magic. The first few minutes I would swim out my daily anxieties and then my mind would move on to more imaginative or spiritual thoughts. Sometimes I just thought about breathing and what a wonder it was that my arms and legs and breathing moved me through the wonderful water in an effortless harmony. Time no longer had any meaning for me. Body surfing, too, brought me into the flow of the Universe, jumping over the waves and into the waves. The most fun is to swim with the wave, let it catch you and carry you into shore. You move through the air and in the water in this smooth partnership of sun, water, salt, and sand. Time does not stand still; it no longer seems to exist. Whoosh. When catching the wave does not work, you are turned inward, you tumble over and over again in the water, not sure which end is up or where the ocean begins and the shore ends. You feel waterlogged, clumsy, and silly.

The circle with which I practice, the Web, is a healing and teaching circle and one of the foundational concepts that we teach is "all time is now." It is often a difficult concept to grasp because we live in a fast-paced, linear world that perceives time as past, present, and future. The past is over and the future is yet to come. Time, though, is a human invention so that humans can contexualize their experiences and provide a frame of reference for their experiences. We invented time so that humans can maintain the concept of past, present, and future.

Nowadays, we are bullied by time, by our own invention. We never have enough time. We treat it like a commodity when we spend time, waste time, or save time. We act as if time is our adversary—we are in a race against time. Time is our ally when the Rolling Stones tell us that "time is on my side." Time is inexorable as time marches on. We feel pressured when we are on a timeline. We relax or get punished in a timeout.

We can change our thinking about time. When we cast a circle and go between the worlds, we go outside of time. If you have read the *Chronicles of Narnia* books by C. S. Lewis you know that time goes on different speeds in different worlds. That is true about the legends of the land of faery, where a mortal is kidnapped and taken to the land of faery and stays there for a year. Upon return, the kidnapped one discovers that a hundred years have passed. If we think about time as a circle rather than a line, we can see that the past, present, and future phase into one another. We can change the past and we can change how the past manifest in our lives.

I recently had an experience in changing the past. A friend of mine told me that one of the most disturbing things he had ever seen as a child was when he saw two big boys from his neighborhood trying to take a dog's eyes out with a spoon. That scene haunted me and disturbed me. It happened nearly forty years ago, so there was not anything I could do about it, but I could not get it out of my heart or out of my mind. One day while I was in the shower, I went into a light meditative state when the warm water washed over me. The mind picture came to me of the two boys, the dog, and the spoon. It was very strange, but familiar, too, like some of the shamanic trance work I have done. I was there and yet I was not there. I could feel the energy of the two boys and I could feel the energy of the dog. I could tell the dog was female but not what breed. I knew she could feel my presence and the boys could not. It might have been good to give them a good scare! I could only use the tools I had, so I sent her a Reiki attunement emphasizing the symbols of energy and emotional healing. When it was over, I felt her burst of energy, gratitude, and love. I have to believe that she found some way to escape. The scene no longer haunts me. I would not have been able to do this if I had been bound by the traditional definitions of past, present, and future.

The Water Maiden needs the perspective of time, particularly the perspective that all time is now, in order to move her from an emotional junkie to a fully mature adult who loves and grieves in perspective.

⚭ Flowing Through Time
A Ritual for the Dark Moon in Pisces

Creating Sacred Space: Spend some time thinking about time and what it means to you. As an experiment, do not wear a watch to work, or spend some time at home with the clocks covered. What are your feelings about time and your activities? And what do you feel about feelings?

Cast the Circle: Walk three times around the circle with a broom or staff, chanting, "A circle is cast, a circle is cast, a circle is cast."

Summon the Guardians and the Elementals:

Summon the West:

> Guardians of the Water Spirits, flow with me into
> the space between the worlds, Undines of water
> creatures, dolphins, fishes and mermaids, swim into
> the space between the worlds. Hail and welcome.

Summon the North:

> Guardians of the Earth Spirits, join me in the space
> between the worlds. Gnomes of the earth creatures,
> worms, rocks and rills, join me in the space between
> the worlds. Hail and welcome.

Summon the East:

> Guardians of the Air Spirits, breeze with me into the
> space between the worlds. Sylphs of the flying ones,
> birds and bats, join me in the space between the
> worlds. Hail and welcome.

Summon the South:

> Guardians of the Fire Spirits, spark with me into the
> space between the worlds, Salamanders of the fire
> and flame, join me in the space between the worlds.
> Hail and welcome.

Evoke the Goddess:

> Aphrodite, goddess of love and emotion, flow into
> my rite and bring your sensuality. Hail and welcome.

Evoke the God:

> Eros, god of love and the interconnectedness of
> being, flow into my rite and bring your emotional
> being. Hail and welcome.

Center and Ground: You are standing next a harbor, a great
rock. Feel that your whole body is a rock. Blend with the rock,

solid, unmovable, secure. Feel the sun reach down, warm you, and embrace you. Feel the gentle sea wash over you, cleansing you and loving you. Feel the solid security of the earth beneath you. You are connected and immovable. You are grounded.

Statement of Ritual Intent:

> Water flows and cleanses us and heals us of our emotion. Time flows and takes us out of time and space, shifting us between the worlds. I flow as I learn to experience the inexplicable melding of mind, emotion, body, and spirit. I ask the spirits to help me learn the joy of flow.

❦ Meditation

You are standing in complete darkness. You look into the sky and see the Lady Moon shift through all of her phases from full to completely dark. You know that the Goddess is smiling on you even though you cannot see her face. You notice you are standing by the water. The water rises in dark waves toward you. The water welcomes you. You are enveloped by a large drop of water. You are inside this drop and completely immersed in the wetness of water. The drop that surrounds you turns RED as you go deeper. The drop that surrounds you turns ORANGE as you go deeper. The drop that surrounds you turns YELLOW as you go deeper. The drop that surrounds you turns GREEN as you go deeper. The drop that surrounds you turns BLUE as you go deeper. The drop that surrounds you turns INDIGO as you go deeper. The drop that surrounds you turns VIOLET as you go deeper. The drop turns CRYSTAL CLEAR as you go deeper.

The drop releases you from its gentle embrace and you find yourself in water, paddling to stay afloat. It is choppy

*and you have some difficulty staying afloat while at the
same time you know you can touch bottom if needed.
Water gets in your mouth. Taste it. As you get tired,
you are buoyed up by the water and carried on the waves.
You relax and stop trying to stay afloat. Relax and let the
water envelop you. Feel it move you gently, gently,
gently. The wave moves up and down in gentle harmony
with your mind as you relax into the water's embrace.
The water moves you gently, gently. Your mind no longer
cares where you are going as the water gently envelops
you. The water speeds up slightly, carrying you in the
waves and you feel your body enveloped, melting further
into the waves. You realize that you are 80 percent water
and you can no longer tell where the water begins and you
end. You are moving to the rhythm of the waves and they
move you gently, gently. You feel the movement deep in
the cells of your body, in the deep recesses of your mind.
You feel your spirit move and merge with the vast watery
bosom of the watery maiden goddess as she whispers to
you. What does she say? Is there something you need to
ask? Ask it. She will merge with you and speak as her
body and yours come together. Her watery embrace heals
you and loves you. Rest in the gentleness of the waves as
the whispering voice of the goddess gives you words of love
and healing. When it is time, the waves will take you back
toward the shore. You feel a gentle separation and you
can tell where your body begins and the water ends. Keep
with you the sense of connection and love. You see the
CRYSTAL CLEAR drop envelop you again as you come
back. You see the drop turn VIOLET as you come back.
You see the drop turn INDIGO as you come back. You
see the drop turn BLUE as you come back. You see the
drop turn GREEN as you come back. You see the drop*

*turn YELLOW as you come back. You see the drop turn
ORANGE as you come back. You see the drop turn RED
as you come back. You are back in yourself in your circle.*

Raising a Cone of Power: Chant this, getting a little faster and
louder. Move and dance as you chant. Clap your hands and flow
around your circle in ecstatic union with all that is.

Time flows and love flows,
Water flows and the goddess flows,
I flow and you flow
As part of the one.
I flow, I flow, flow flow flow flow
FLOW FLOW FLOWWWWWWWW.

Cakes and Ale: Say a prayer of thanksgiving to all the spirits
who swam with you in this ritual.

Center and Ground: You are the rock next to the harbor, solid
and unmoving. As the water flows over you, feel yourself change
back into your body. Keep with you that feeling of the love of
nature. You are grounded and back into yourself.

Farewell to the God:

Eros, God of Love, thank you for your love and the
wisdom of love. Thank you for your presence in my
rite. Go with my thanks and my blessings. Hail and
well met.

Farewell to the Goddess:

Loving Aphrodite, thank you for your passion and
your presence in my rite. Go with my thanks and my
blessings. Hail and well met.

Farewell to the Guardians and Elementals:

Dismiss the South:

Guardians of the South, thank you for the focus of
will, the passion of intent. Salamanders, thank you

for the fire of love. Guardians and Salamanders, go with my thanks and my blessings. Hail and well met.

Dismiss the East:

Guardians of the East, thank you for clarity and for vision. Sylphs, thank you for the breath of life. Guardians and Sylphs, go with my thanks and my blessings. Hail and well met.

Dismiss the North:

Guardians of the North, thank you for the solid rock of security. Gnomes, thank you for the deep and the dark. Guardians and Gnomes, go with my thanks and my blessings. Hail and well met.

Dismiss the West:

Guardians of the West, thank you for loving and life. Undines, thank you for the heart of the matter. Guardians and Undines, go with my thanks and my blessings. Hail and well met.

Open the Circle: Moving widdershins, chant.
The circle is open but unbroken. Blessed be.

෴

Dark Moon in Aries

The dance of the Dark Moon Path continues its inward spiral with the spark of the fire sign of Aries. Fire is a spark in Aries, ignites a flame in Leo, and becomes a wildfire in Sagittarius. Aries is a Maiden driven by the fire of her assertion of identity. Who am I? I am She, the Fire Maiden.

The symbol of Aries is the ram, which typified both a heroic and a combative nature to the ancient Greeks. Jason traveled with the Argonauts to redeem the Golden Fleece. In the process he did heroic things and fought battles. He enlisted the assistance of Medea, who used her considerable magical powers to aid him. She did not use her powers for good and took advantage of him—

two strong-minded, powerful people locked in a battle of love and anger, with both showing an incredible strength of will.

Aries is strong-willed, stubborn, confident, clear thinking, and innovating. There is a straightforward exuberance about Aries so that creativity sparks and sparkles. This can lead to stubbornness that is mulish, arrogant, and headstrong. An Aries will express an opinion clearly and confidently, and will not listen to alternate opinions, stating firmly, "This is it, that is the way it is—case closed." Aries can be reckless, rash, uncooperative, irresponsible, rude, and argumentative. Magnificent strengths have difficult faults.

Aries is a fire sign. Fire can burn us and fire can warm us. Fire transforms us, fire cooks our food, and it can reduce forests to ashes. Fire works with water to temper metal. The gods jealously guarded fire. When Prometheus defied Zeus and gave fire to humankind, he was punished by Zeus. He had Prometheus bound to a rock and had his intestines picked out by buzzards. Every day his intestines were renewed so that they could be picked out again in eternal torture—an incredible punishment for giving fire to humans. Does possessing the ability to create and use fire make a person somehow divine? Is that why Zeus was so angry and vengeful? Yes? Fire enhances life, changes life, and destroys life. It does sound like part of a job description for a god or goddess, doesn't it?

When the sun is in Aries, pagans celebrate one of the quarter holidays, the vernal equinox. This is the festival that celebrates the day that is one-half night and one-half light. Plants are shooting out of the soil and reaching for the sun. The life that began underground is now visible to the eye. It is an adolescent celebration of joy, the joy of growth and the power of health and youth. Adolescence can be an unthinking time, a time to revel in growing things and exploring new sensations. This can drive the adolescent to do weird, dangerous, stupid, and hurtful things.

A coworker who had survived raising sons to manhood once told me that men from the ages of fifteen to twenty-four had the best reflexes they would ever have in their lives. She then added, "And that is because they have to have them."

The Fire Maiden is youthful exuberance, confidence, and spirit. She sparkles with her cleverness and she can wound with her selfishness. The person who personifies the Fire Maiden to me is Bette Midler, in her career during the 1970s and 1980s. She is an enormously talented woman who does not have conventional beauty. She does not really need it because she has talent and style. Her humor during the years mentioned was broad, ribald, subtle, outrageous, and very funny. She has made some good movies and some bad movies, because even sparkling creativity fizzles sometimes. When she announced the award for best song at the Academy Awards show, she tripped out in an incredibly ugly dress. It was so ugly that it was interesting and funky. She did not walk to the microphone; she fluttered, sashayed, smirked, and grinned. She lifted the hem of her dress and said, "Okay, let's hear it for the dress!" She then proceeded to announce the songs in what was obviously an unscripted commentary that was both funny and critical of the songs at the same time.

The Fire Maiden is outrageous and not overly concerned with the opinions of others, although she loves others deeply and greatly. She is carried through life by the fire of her passion and she survives by the power of her will. She may be headstrong, but she is also heartstrong. She lives the life of the soul and is a pioneer, going forward where no one else will. When she hears someone say that is where angels fear to tread, she replies, "Phh-hht, those angels are wimps anyway. Let's go!" We will follow her because she lights the way with her sense of herself and her joy of life.

Her sense of identity and confidence in it is what gives the Fire Maiden her spirited life. Who we are and how we feel about who we are becomes very important and influences how we conduct our lives. Having a clear view of who we are, what are our strengths and what are our faults, helps us to be fully human. I once said to a coworker that the world works differently for people based on how they feel about themselves. I got an incredulous look. Think about it. If you think you are an ugly person, you may project that thinking to others and you may feel disregarded and thus deprive yourself of a social life. You may feel you have to settle. Regardless of how you actually look compared to conventional standards of beauty, if you are confident you will have people holding you in high regard and valuing you. Some self-defense training for women includes information on posture and attitude that projects to criminals "Here is a victim." There is a funny scene in the movie *Crossing Delancy* where the main character's elderly grandmother is getting some self-defense training and we see the entire class of elderly, frail old ladies is walking straight and tall and shouting, "I am confident, I am not a victim!"

Who you are is important. In many pagan and Wiccan circles we say "You are God, you are Goddess." Identity is important in the life of the soul. The magic we practice is one of the ways of asserting our identity as a divine being and understanding that the Divine is inside us as well as outside of us. When we look at ourselves it is with the eyes of the Divine. We should look at ourselves with the eyes of love. We need to add compassion. The Fire Maiden says, "I am." In her enthusiasm, she may forget there are others, and say, "I am the only one." By looking at herself with the eyes of love and compassion she becomes a passionate, mature woman with the will to live the life of passion and soul. Then the Fire Maiden loves life and loves others.

♈ I Am
A Ritual for the Dark Moon in Aries

Creating Sacred Space: A few days before the ritual, spend some time listing your roles in life: wife, daughter, son, boss, gay, straight, mother, father, teacher, and so forth. Then write out the qualities that you exhibit in these roles: assertive, fun, shy, and sloppy. Be honest but don't be cruel. Take one hundred pennies (match sticks, marbles, etc), which represents your entire wealth. Look at the qualities and think about how much you would pay to keep them. This is where you invest your thinking and the profit or loss is your identity. What would you change? What would you keep the same? Keep the important ones with you for the ritual. Bring a mirror to the ritual.

Cast the Circle: Walk three times around the circle with a candle (lit or unlit), chanting, "A circle is cast."

Summon the Guardians and the Elementals:

Summon the North:

> Sages and Crones of the North, Guardians of the
> deep silence and the magic of the world, join me in
> my sacred circle. Gnomes, burrowers in the dark, join
> me in my rite. Hail and welcome.

Summon the East:

> Maidens and Youth of the Mind, Guardians of the
> Intellect, join me in my sacred circle. Sylphs, gentle
> breath of air, join me in my sacred circle. Hail and
> welcome.

Summon the South:

> Amazons and Warriors of the South, Guardians of
> the Will, join me in my sacred circle. Salamanders,
> creatures of fire, join me in my sacred circle. Hail and
> welcome.

Summon the West:

> Mothers and Lovers of the West, Guardians of the
> Heart, join me in my sacred circle. Undines, Divers
> into the deep well of love, join me in my sacred
> circle. Hail and welcome.

Evoke the Goddess:

> Lady Artemis, Swift Lady of the Hunt, Join me in
> my rite and bring me the surety of self. Hail and
> welcome.

Evoke the God:

> Prometheus, God Unbound, join me in my rite and
> bring me the gift of generosity and sacrifice. Hail and
> welcome.

Center and Ground: You are a tree standing on the edge of a
forest. Send your root down into the heart of Mother Earth. Find
a rock and anchor your root there. Pull energy up into yourself,
feeling the energy surge through your body and your extremities.
Feel the energy go up through your crown and reach out toward
the energy of the Universe. Feel the flow of the Universe pulse
toward you and meet in an embrace. You are grounded, connected to the Universe and to Mother Earth.

Statement of Ritual Intent:

> I have invested in myself and I am confident that I
> am valuable to myself. I am asking the spirits to give
> me a true picture of myself and celebrate who I am.

☙ Meditation

> *Settle yourself comfortably and breathe out three times,*
> *with the third exhale coming out as OMMMMMMM.*
> *Hold the mirror out in front of you so that you can see as*
> *much of yourself as possible. Drink in the vision of your-*

self. Look at yourself as a collection of skin and bones and hair. Bring the mirror closer and look at yourself as a collection of fine qualities: honest eyes, noble nose, kindness, and so forth. Close your eyes and see the mirror before you. See the mirror grow to life size before your eyes. Put your hands on the edges and step over the threshold of the mirror. Step three steps further inside. Look around the world of the mirror and notice what the landscape is like. See another person in front of you in this land of the mirror. Walk up to the figure and see that the figure is You. You. See how wonderful you are. Greet You. Walk around the back of You. Drink in the image of You. As you look at the image of You, discover the inner qualities of You. Stand in front of YOU and tell YOUR-SELF what you know about your qualities and how you invest in YOUrself. Ask YOU what is needed to see yourself truly and lovingly. Ask what you need to grow and what you need to gain the outrageous joy of I AM. Listen. When the time is ready, ask if there are any final words or gift YOU has for you. Put out your hand and receive the gift. Look down in your hand and see that you have a gift for YOU. Give it to YOU. Say goodbye and walk back the way you came. You will see the edges of the mirror. Put your hands on the outside edges and step over the threshold. See the mirror shrink to its usual size. Open your eyes and look into the mirror. Smile and say, "I AM."

Raise the Cone of Power: Stand up and start to dance around the circle. Clap your hands and jump up and down. Sing the words or chant the words, getting louder and faster until the crescendo whoosh of power.

I AM I AM I AM I AM I AM
I I I I I I AMMMMMMMMMM

Cakes and Ale: Say a prayer of thanksgiving for yourself and your qualities. Thank the spirit for being a part of your ritual and your life.

Center and Ground: You are back as the tree. Gently disconnect your energy flowing to and from the Universe. Take what you need and know that the energy of the Universe is always there and there for you. Gently untangle your anchoring root and draw it up to yourself. Keep what energy you need and ground the rest. You are centered and grounded in the love of the Earth and the Universe.

Farewell to the God:

> Prometheus, God who gave Fire, thank you for your
> generosity and sacrifice. Go with my thanks and my
> blessings. Hail and well met.

Farewell to the Goddess:

> Artemis, Lady of the Woods, thank you for your
> swift wit and generosity. Go with my thanks and my
> blessings. Hail and well met.

Farewell to the Guardians and the Elementals:

Farewell to the West:

> Guardians of my Heart, thank you for the wisdom of
> love. Go with my thanks and my blessings. Hail and
> well met.

Farewell to the South:

> Guardians of my Passion, thank you for the ability to
> achieve. Go with my thanks and my blessings. Hail
> and well met.

Farewell to the East:

> Guardians of my Mind, thank you for the ability
> to think and discern. Go with my thanks and my
> blessings. Hail and well met.

Farewell to the North:

> Guardians of my Wisdom, thank you for the ability
> to know and understand. Go with my thanks and my
> blessings. Hail and well met.

Open the Circle: With your candle, walk widdershins around
the circle, chanting, "The circle is open and unbroken." At the
end, blow out the flame and say, "Blessed be."

❧

Dark Moon in Taurus

The next step on the Dark Moon Path is onto the rich soil of the earth sign Taurus. Taurus is the soil that makes the mountains rise in Virgo and the earth quake in Capricorn. The Earth Maiden is deeply connected to the Earth and to the body of the Goddess.

The bull symbolizes the earth sign of Taurus. The bull is one of the ancient symbols of fertility and power. Throughout the Mediterranean, the bull was the consort of the earth goddess. The bull was the sacred animal of the god of the seas, Poseidon, whose symbol was a large black bull. The goddess culture on the island of Crete revered the bull. Men and women performed bull dances by tumbling and jumping off the running bull as a tribute to the power of the Goddess. The king of Crete, Minos, prayed for a bull to sacrifice, since none of his herd was worthy of sacrifice to the gods. The gods sent him a beautiful white bull that came from the waves of the sea. It was so beautiful that Minos hid the bull in his own herd and sacrificed another to the sea god. Poseidon became enraged and caused Minos' wife to become enamored of the bull. She mated with the bull and had a son, half-man and half-bull, called the Minotaur.

People born with the sign of Taurus are stable, loyal, and steadfast friends—someone on whom you can rely and who will be patient and industrious. Taureans are practical, prudent, resourceful, and consistent. Taurus people feel things deeply, so they love long and they hate long. They never forget and they can be bullheaded, and stuck in a rut. Taurus personalities create new definitions for adhering doggedly to the status quo and take stubbornness to new heights. Strong in groundedness can grow strong into stubbornness.

Pagans, goddess-worshipers, Wiccans, and others believe that the earth is the body of the Goddess. Think about all the different kinds of soil. There is clay, beach sand, black soil, red soil, desert sand, rocky soil, and scree. Plants grow in all these kinds of soil, regardless of the nutrients the soil may or may not have. All soil nurtures things so that they can grow. We may not always see the beauty of the things that grow.

I spent most of my life in Maryland where the spring, my favorite season, is flowery, graceful, beautiful, and long. There is a fragrance in the air and flower petals on the ground. In my late thirties, I moved to the southern tier of New York State, which is stark and mountainous. Spring was late and it was a struggle for things to get to the surface and to grow. There was a stark, rugged beauty to the spring that I did not see for a long time. It is a very different type of beauty.

When the sun is in Taurus, pagans celebrate the holiday of Beltane. Beltane is the ancient holiday of fertility and joy. It is the time when agricultural societies plow the fields and plant them. It is a celebration of the union of soil, water, sun, and seed. It is about fertilizing the fields. The human part of that is the celebration of human fertility, of sex. It is the union of man and woman in the joy of their bodies and the creation of life. It is a lustful holiday. One of my teachers was fond of saying, "Beltane is not just a holiday, it is a state of mind." The state of mind is not only of lust and pursuit of union but of the merging of one with another and the synergy of energy. It is an earthy celebration of our physical nature. The negative side of Beltane is obsession with sexual matters, particularly sexual jealousy, sexual obsession, and indiscriminate, predatory sexual behavior. While Beltane celebrates the delights of carnal life, the Dark side obsesses about sex and preys on others.

The Earth Maiden lives the life of the body. She has a sense that everything moves together as part of a unified whole. She is exuberant as well as stubborn. She is a confident woman with a robust sense of worth. Part of that sense of worth comes from a respect and love for her body. She knows the truth of the Charge of the Goddess, "All acts of pleasure and love are My rituals."

Our bodies are a part of our connection to the natural world and to the Goddess. According to Genesis, Jehovah made the first man, Adam, from clay. The words of funerals tell us we go from "dust to dust." After we die, we become earth again. Our bodies come from earth. They come from the body of the Goddess and they come from the bodies of mothers, and our bodies are a direct product of mingling of bodies of our fathers and mothers. Coming from a sacred source, we should treat them as a sacred thing to be honored, celebrated, and enjoyed. Saint Paul said that "you are the temple of the living God," and surely that implies that your physical being as the temple houses what is sacred: you. To honor and worship something means to use it as it was intended, and to tend it as was intended. Intention depends on tending.

One of the teachers I studied with briefly said that she really did not like to be incarnate so she spent a lot of time on the astral plane. She was deeply resistant to being in her body. I think she was resistant to being in the here-and-now. I experienced her as flighty, disorganized, and difficult to pin down. It was difficult to learn from her, but since I really wanted to learn from her I worked hard to learn. What I did learn was profound and not the least of what I learned was the value of being grounded.

The Earth Maiden celebrates the connection to the earth and to the body of the Goddess. She enjoys the pleasures of the body, including eating, drinking, sex, and sensation. Often the media bombards us with images that tell us our body is unacceptable and we learn to hate our bodies. The Earth Maiden may then become neurotic and abuse herself. It is by accepting herself as she is that the Earth Maiden becomes a joyful, connected woman, expressing herself with and through her body.

℞ Let's Get Physical
A Ritual for the Dark Moon in Taurus

Creating Sacred Space: Spend some time thinking about what gives you pleasure. Then think about your body. Think about your favorite body parts and what you like about your body. Look at your body and tell yourself what you like about each part of you. Be specific and detailed; include your eyebrows, lips, toes, butt, toenails, and so on. If there is a part of your body that you do not like, say "I do not like my _____," and leave it at that. Say this out loud before the ritual.

Cast the Circle: Use your body to cast the circle. Walk, skip, run, or hop. Use your arms. Three times and a circle is cast.

Summon the Guardians and the Directions: Begin with the North and summon the Guardians and the Elementals in your own words. At the end of each phrase, say, "By the body of the Goddess, I bid you welcome."

Evoke the Goddess:

> Gaia, Goddess on whose body we walk, join me
> in my rite and bring me the delight of physical
> presence. Hail and welcome.

Evoke the God:

> Hades, God of the Underworld, where we will go,
> join me in my rite and bring me the realization that
> all is one and all is eternal. Hail and welcome.

Center and Ground: You are a large rock in the mountains. Feel the silent peace of the mountains and draw that into the being. Feel the gravel beneath you and feel your rockness merge with the gravel and the earth below that. Feel your consciousness go deep into the rocky soil. Know that you are firmly situated in the mountain bosom of the Mother Earth. Feel the sun warm your rocky back and feel the warm embrace of the sun envelop you.

Ritual Intent:

> We are incarnate beings, in specific bodies. This
> body. My body. My body is a joy to me and others
> should see it in my step, in my smile, and in me.
> My body is a temple that houses the sacred Me. My
> body is sacred and every way I use it is a prayer and
> a ritual.

Activity: Stand comfortably in the circle. You are standing before the God and Goddess and all the Spirit Guardians of this world and the next. They are the witness and sharers of your celebration of your body. Name each part of your body in blessing. If you come to a part that is a problem for you just say, "Blessed is/are my _____."

    Blessed are my toes because they keep me balanced
    Blessed are my feet because _____
    Blessed are my _____ because _____
    Blessed are my _____ because _____
    Blessed are my _____ because _____
    Blessed are my _____ because _____

Raising the Cone of Power: Chant or sing the words below, get louder and faster and dance around the circle saying and shouting, "My name!" until the power crescendos into the Universe:

    Blessed am I, blessed am I
    Blessed am I, blessed am I
    Blessed am I
    My name, My name!

Cakes and Ale: Say a prayer of thanksgiving for you, for your body, and for the sacred attention of yourself and of the Universe.

Center and Ground: You are the rock in the mountain. Gently move your consciousness back into the rock. Move away from the Mother Earth. Leave the embrace of the sun. Know that you can return to this comfort and power any time you want. Be conscious of your blessed body as you come back to the here and now.

Farewell to the God:

    Hades, Lord of the Dark Underground, thank you for your wisdom in my rite. Go with my thanks and my blessings. Hail and farewell.

Farewell to the Goddess:

> Gaia, Mother of our bodies, thank you for your
> kindness in my rite. Go with my thanks and my
> blessing. Hail and farewell.

Dismiss the Guardians and the Elementals: Using similar words when you summoned the Guardians and the directions, thank them for their presence and by the body of the Goddess, bid them farewell.

Open the Circle: Going widdershins, open the circle with your body. Run, skip, sing, and dance.

The circle is open and blessed be.

ႆ

The Synergy of the Maiden

The Goddess as Maiden is an independent, dedicated woman. She is often unthinking as she follows her life. The Air Maiden, the Water Maiden, the Fire Maiden, and the Earth Maiden are all part of the whole picture of the Maiden Goddess. You do not have to be one or the other. Just as the Goddess is a whole being, so are you. You may follow the life of the mind and add physical activity and follow your spiritual path with your heart and soul. The Maiden Goddess as a mature being follows her star with all of her being—including heart, mind, body, and soul.

Synergy combines component energies and creates a whole that is greater than all of its parts. Then it changes the world, the Universe, and the person. No one part is more important than the other. You are the Maiden as well, and the Mother, the Crone, and the Weaver. At this time, you may be emphasizing one more than the other. In your unique way, you take the strengths and passions of the Maiden and combine her into your being and into your life as part of all that is.

The Dark Mother

The Dark Mother

The Dark Moon Path deepens as we approach the Goddess as the Mother. We see the Full Moon as the Mother. The round bright moon reminds us of the round, full belly of a pregnant woman and we see the exciting promise of fertility and the joy of bringing new life into the world.

The word "mother" evokes many different emotions in us. We love our mothers, we hate our mothers, and some of us do not know our mothers. We have been mothered and we have not been mothered. We fear mothering and call it smothering. We have been bereft of mothering and felt abandoned. Some of us have birthed children out of our bodies, some of us have not. Some of us have mothered other people's children; some of us have mothered ourselves. Regardless of our experience of mothering, every one of us has lain in the womb next to the heart of the mother. Each of us has had a woman's body feed us and protect us. Each of us has experienced the body of another by being inside that body. For months, we are carried in that body and experience the physicalness of that body. We also experience the emotions as we lie in the amniotic fluid. We live in the rhythm of the mother, whatever that rhythm may be.

We approach the Mother Goddess, seeking her rhythms. As we go through the lunar year on the Dark Moon Path, we experience the richness of the mother as the Air Mother, the Water Mother, the Fire Mother, and the Earth Mother. Each gives us a new perspective on the mother. The breath becomes the wind in Gemini. The drop becomes a stream in Cancer. The spark becomes a flame in Leo. The soil becomes a mountain in Virgo.

We tend to idealize the Mother and then demand that our mothers follow this ideal. We have images of a pioneer mother with a gun in one hand and a baby on her hip, forging a new country. We have Beaver's mother vacuuming the house in high heels, wearing a beautifully ironed dress and a lovely strand of pearls. We have the *Brady Bunch* mother smiling while raising six—count 'em—somewhat bland children to play on an artificial turf lawn.

The Goddess Mother stories are not so easy or idealized. Demeter plunges the whole world into darkness and winter when separated from her daughter. Kali Ma loves and destroys. Hera, a mother herself, seeks to destroy the children of her philandering husband.

We then weave the Dark into this Mother and we find the Dark Mother. We are not talking about an Evil Mother but a mother who understands that the Dark is with us. She understands that the pain of labor brings forth a miracle, a baby. She understands that the cute little baby brings a lifetime of responsibility, joy, pain, and worry. Like the Dark Maiden, it is understanding that brings the Mother into the Dark.

CR

Dark Moon in Gemini

The Dark Moon Path continues its inward journey into Gemini, an air sign. The breath of air from Aquarius is now a wind in Gemini and will become a storm in Libra. As we move deeper into the Dark, we greet the Mother Goddess.

The picture of Gemini is that of twins. According to Greek myth, the twins of the Zodiac were Castor and Pollux, two people who looked so much alike that they became twins and they loved each other so much that they were twins in their hearts. Pollux was the immortal son of Zeus while Castor was mortal. When Castor was killed, Pollux could not accompany him to the land of the dead. Pollux mourned so greatly that Zeus allowed them to alternate every six months, spending six months in the land of the dead and six months in heaven. Unfortunately, Castor was in heaven, and Pollux was in the land of the dead. They were not together but both were allowed to experience spiritual heaven and mortal death. Castor and Pollux were twinned in partnership and in love.

In Roman myth, the twins Romulous and Remus were twins divided by fate. They were the sons of Rhea Silvia, a vestal virgin seduced by Mars, the God of War. Her father's rival, King Amulius, fearing the boys would take his throne, had the boys placed in a basket and thrown into the Tiber River. The boys were washed ashore and discovered by a she-wolf who nursed them. Later a shepherd found them and raised the boys with his own children. When they became adults, the twins discovered their true identity. They overthrew Amulius and restored their grandfather to the throne. They then set out to found their own city.

As they traveled, Romulous and Remus quarreled over where they should found their own city. They decided that whoever saw the largest number of vultures in flight would decide where the city should be started. Romulous saw twelve vultures in flight, and declared that was a sign that the gods wanted him to decide where the new city should be. Remus saw only six vultures and accused his brother of cheating. In the ensuing argument, Remus was killed and Romulous founded and ruled the city of Rome. Romulous and Remus were twinned in conflict and in hate.

Twins have fascinated people from the beginning. In the days when successful pregnancies and live children were not always taken for granted, a successful twin birth was a double miracle. Today, both science and psychology do special studies of twins, of their biology, of their psychology and their socialization. Frequently reported in the media are stories about twins, separated at birth, who have made similar choices in spouses, careers, and lifestyles. Years ago, my mother was the teacher of twins. The two girls were in separate classes, as was the policy in those days. When they celebrated their birthday, each gave the other the same present and the same card. You could say this happened because they were raised together and knew each other's taste, or you could say that they shared a mystical bond.

Do we long for that kind of sympathy and connection with another soul? Are we perplexed by it, fascinated by it, or repulsed by it? There is also the legend of the evil twin, where one twin is pure and good and the other twin is purely evil. I joke about it myself. My middle name is Gail and I am very insistent on being called by my middle name. I am rarely called by my first name, Susan, calling her my evil twin. I always assign my mistakes, inappropriate remarks, and problems to that awful Susan person.

In astrology, Gemini is portrayed as bright, intelligent, studious, and rational. The inward spiral of Gemini is someone who is flighty, gossipy, shallow, and superficial. Geminis are often seen as people with a double personality, a dark side and a light side. We often see the Mother as a dual personality as well. Gemini brings us our first experience of the Goddess as the Mother. As Gemini, she is the Air Mother. Air is the element that can be a gentle breeze that cools us or the fierce wind that blows everything away.

The Air Mother is rational and intellectual. She can use her strong mind and tongue to praise and to scold. She uses words to cut away the crap and get to the heart of the matter. With a sharp mind and tongue, she tells us what is what and takes no prisoners. She also uses that mind and tongue to solve problems and to praise us for our strengths. The altruism of the Air Maiden becomes an Air Mother who tells truths, regardless of the feelings those truths might wound. Anyone who has been sliced and diced by the Air Mother's keen insights may not see the loving intent behind the words. Conversely, the Air Mother in her relentless quest for truth may not see the wounds inflicted with her words. Like the Air Maiden, the Air Mother needs the awareness of others to temper her words and deliver her messages in ways that can be heard by those who then become willing to listen.

One avenue to compassion is knowledge, the province of Gemini. The life of the mind is an exciting life. Learning, study-ing, researching, and writing are all part of the life of the mind. Living the life of the mind means that you use all your critical faculties to analyze and evaluate information. I spent many years in graduate school and working in academia. I was and am excit-ed by the life of the mind. I get to write, think, and be an expert in my chosen fields of study and work. To research something is to search and pursue a thought until you find it. You evaluate its validity, you examine it from all sides and then, if you are lucky, you come up with a new aspect, a new way of looking at the thought or a new application of the thought. Then it becomes yours. The process and the ownership of ideas is heady and absorbing. The next step in this process is to communicate your excitement to others. When your students learn to think and then move forward to become experts in their own areas, the circle becomes complete, because then the student teaches the teacher.

Flip the coin of strength and you see a weakness. Someone living the life of the mind can become overly intellectual, arro-gant, and unemotional, forgetting that experience and emotions are important teachers. Many years ago, I was in group therapy where I was asked to describe my feelings about something. I processed my feelings so quickly into thought that I could not even say, "I feel." I could only say, "I think." At the time I did not get it at all, even though the other members of the group were very quick to point out that I was thinking and not feeling. I was not living in my emotions at all. I was living all in my head. Ultimately, it was confusing and I was bewildered about people and emotions. When I learned to balance my mind with my spirit and my emotions, I became much more centered.

We need our minds. We are blessed to be living in an era with an enormous amount of data that is thrown at us in a multitude of forms and media. We need our minds to make that data relevant (information) and we need our minds to make that information relevant in our lives (knowledge). What you do not know can hurt you. Ignorance is not bliss, nor is ignorance an excuse. Ignorance is costly. We all need to be smart. We need to be smart about everything.

We need to be smart about our spirituality. I have had several of what I call "bogus occult experiences." These experiences have been as harmless as attending an open group, which said it was open to new members, but no one spoke to me and people moved away from me when I sat down. Others have been as harmful as spending five years in a spiritual group that controlled every aspect of my life from sleeping hours, to money, to sex, and to where I worked. I could have been smarter. Instead of blaming myself for not being smart enough, I spent time thinking about these experiences so that I could understand the world and myself better. It was not particularly easy or pleasant to see myself in the mirror of those experiences, but it was important to understand the value of those experiences. Those experiences have shaped who I am and how I perceive the world.

It is important to integrate mind with the rest of us—body, emotion, and soul. We can live a life of the mind, be quite successful, and have an interesting and productive life. Choosing to do so can mean choosing to ignore other aspects of ourselves. You can bet that if you ignore something in this lifetime, you will work on that in the next lifetime. I recently read a lawyer-in-distress novel called *The Tenth Justice* (Brad Meltzer, Warner Books, 1998). In it, the supercilious, arrogant Chief Justice tells the bright young law clerk that those who feel see life as a tragedy. Those who think see life as a comedy, obviously intending for the smart-aleck young lawyer to see thinking as a preferred way of life. "Of course," replied the young lawyer, "for those who can sing, life is a musical."

The Air Mother is a teacher, holding us to a high standard and relentlessly challenging us to be our best. She brings a brilliant intellect to our aid. Combined with heart and soul, the Air Mother sings with joy.

♋ My Twin
A Ritual for the Dark Moon in Gemini

Creating Sacred Space: Sometimes we may feel that we are a mass of contradictions, confusing not only to others but also to ourselves. Spend some time thinking about qualities about yourself that contradict one another. Do not be overly judgmental; these qualities can be "good" or "bad" qualities. Find objects that represent these contradictions or write the qualities on cards. Divide those qualities into two piles. Name those two piles. One is you and one is your twin. You can create an evil twin-good twin dynamic; you can just name them Remus and Romulus, for example, or you can say this is my artistic self, this is my work self. How do you divide yourself?

Cast the Circle: Use your mind to cast the circle. Visualize a light blue circle around you and your sacred space. Then visualize a dark blue circle around you and your sacred space, and finally, visualize indigo around you and your sacred space. Please note that I chose these colors because blue is the color of the East for me. If you use different colors, just be sure they go from lightest to darkest. How these circles position themselves is up to you, I visualize them as very close together surrounding my sacred space. "A circle is cast in the darkness of Air."

Summon the Guardians and the Elementals:

Summon the East:

> Dark blue guardians of our minds and our rational
> selves, guard the airy gate of the East and be
> welcome to my sacred circle. Airy Sylphs of the
> Eastern sky, join me in my sacred circle and blow
> away the cobwebs from my mind.

Summon the South:

> Dark red guardians of our passions and of our will,
> guard the fiery gate of the South and be welcome to
> my sacred circle. Fiery Salamanders of the Southern
> world, burn away the doubts in my mind and
> be welcome to my sacred circle.

Summon the West:

> Dark green guardians of our loves and hates, guard
> the watery West and be welcome to my sacred circle.
> Watery Undines of Western waters, wash away the
> confusion of my mind and be welcome to my sacred
> circle.

Summon the North:

> Dark brown guardians of the earthy rocks and soil,
> guard the earthen gate of the North and join me in
> my sacred circle. Earth Gnomes of silence and the
> dark, bury my self-criticisms in your earth and be
> welcome to my sacred circle.

Evoke the Goddess:

> Lovely Iris, Rainbow woman, messenger of the Gods,
> join me in my rite. Bring the wisdom of communica-
> tion and knowledge and the beauty of the rainbow
> and be welcome to my sacred circle.

Evoke the God:

> Zephyrus, God of the West Wind, join me in my
> rite. Bring with you the gentle breezes of change,
> emotion, and understanding and be welcome to my
> sacred circle.

Center and Ground: You are standing on the edge of the forest, you are a sapling tree. Send your roots deep into the Mother Earth. Feel her warmth and gentleness. Anchor your roots on a rock that you find there, knowing that you are firmly connected to the mother. Send your branches up into the air. Feel the breezes gently rock you. Reach upward and embrace the sky, the Universe of Love. Feel the energy of the Universe reach down and embrace you. There you are embraced by the Love of the Sky and rooted in the Love of Mother Earth.

Statement of Ritual Intent:

> We are beings blessed with a mind. Sometimes our
> thinking and our feeling leads us to feel confused and
> split in two. Who are we really? How can I live with
> thoughts that contradict one another? I will journey
> within myself to find the split, to meet my twin and
> to embrace my twin. We are who we are. So get to
> know who you are.

ଓ Meditation

*Breathe in and out and center yourself. Be comfortable
and in a light trance state. You are standing in the Dark.
Before you are two piles of paper. You realize those are
the qualities you wrote down earlier. Concentrate on one
pile and see it grow life-sized before you. The pile takes
shape and becomes your twin. That mirror image of you
is not you. Look at the other pile and see it grow life-
sized. It moves and envelops you. You are those qualities*

*that you identified and more. More information comes to
you about yourself. Listen carefully to that information.
Turn now and face your twin. See your twin as the
qualities you named earlier and more. See all that your
twin is. Do not judge yourself or your twin. Your twin
stretches out two arms and asks for an embrace.
Embrace your twin and dance together. See how you
fit together and how you move together—one seemingly
so different, yet so much the same. See yourselves fit
together as two pieces of a puzzle and how you complete
each other. Merge closer until you are one. Feel the
rightness of the merging and see strengths become
weaknesses and weaknesses become strengths. See how
it is all part of the One, the You. You may wish to
disconnect from your twin or you may wish to return
from the meditation as a merged self. It is up to you.
Stand while you decide. Whatever you do, thank your
other self for the connection and the disconnection. Sometimes we learn as much from what we are not as we learn
from what we are. Take two breaths and return to the
here and now. Take one more breath and open your eyes.*

Raise the Cone of Power: Take your two piles of yourself and
merge them together. Remember what you named them and
begin to chant those names one after the other, over and over
again. Say it so fast you cannot distinguish between the names.
Start to move in rhythm with your chant, getting louder and
faster until you feel the cone of power WHOOOSH into the
universe.

Cakes and Ale: Say a prayer of thanksgiving for your mind, for
your self, and for your teachers.

Center and Ground: Go back to that sapling tree, young and
growing. Feel the sap course through your body. Send your consciousness down to the roots and the anchor. Gently, ever so

gently disconnect the root from the anchor, knowing that you can always connect with the Love of the Mother. Cast your consciousness upward to the sky. Gently, ever so gently, disconnect yourself from the Universe, knowing that you can always connect with the Love of All that is. You are whole within yourself, grounded and connected.

Dismiss the God:

Zephyrus, God of the Winds, thank you for the wisdom of thought, clarity of vision, and joy of living. Thank you for your presence in my sacred rite. Go with my thanks and my blessings. Hail and farewell.

Dismiss the Goddess:

Delightful Iris, colorful goddess of the freshness of the new day, thank you for your presence in my sacred rite. Go with my thanks and my blessings. Hail and farewell.

Dismiss the Guardians and the Elementals:

Dismiss the North:

Burrowers in the Dark, elementals of the ground and underground, and Guardians of the soil and rock, thank you all for your presence in my sacred rite. Go with my thanks and my blessings. Hail and farewell.

Dismiss the West:

Swimmers of the watery depths and Guardians of the wave and water, thank you for your presence in my sacred rite. Go with my thanks and my blessings. Hail and farewell.

Dismiss the South:

Creatures of the fire and the noonday sun and Guardians of the burning passion, thank you for your presence in my sacred rite. Go with my thanks and my blessings. Hail and farewell.

Dismiss the East:

Creatures of the air, flying ones and Guardians of the breeze and storm, thank you for your presence in my sacred rite. Go with my thanks and my blessings. Hail and farewell.

Open the Circle: Visualize the circle you cast and with your mind see it disappear, going clockwise around the circle. When it is all gone, the circle is open, but unbroken. Blessed be!

༶

Dark Moon in Cancer

The Dark Moon Path dives into the watery emotional sign of Cancer, the sign of hearth and home. Water was a drop in Pisces and is now a stream in Cancer and will become a tidal wave in Scorpio.

The astrological symbol of Cancer is the Crab. The crab was a creature belonging to Hera, the Greek goddess of domestic stability and the wife of Zeus, the philandering king of the gods. Hera was intensely jealous of her husband's liaisons and very hostile to the resulting offspring. Whether Zeus' partners consented or not, Hera was angry, vengeful, and horrifically punitive towards them and their children. When Hercules, one of these offspring, was locked in a battle with the monster

57

Hydra, Hera sent the crab to bite his heel to distract him in a way that would get him killed. The crab bit his heel, held on, and could not be shaken from the assigned task. Even though Hercules killed the monster, Hera placed the crab in the heavens in gratitude for its loyalty.

The crab is an excellent symbol for the qualities of Cancer. Crabs have a hard, nearly impenetrable shell on the outside and are soft and delicate on the inside. If you see crabs walk, you will notice that they walk sideways. Crabs never go directly to their destination; they walk to their destination in a sideways and circuitous path that is not clear to the observer. You can characterize this as subtle or frustrating, or both. Crabs are also scavengers, bottom-feeders who eat the discarded and the dead. Like mothers everywhere, they are picking up after others.

Cancer people nest, creating comfort and a home, all the while searching for and fighting for domestic stability. Like Hera, Cancerians are very insistent on domestic stability, to the point of vengeance when perceiving a threat to their nest. Cancer people are nurturing and protective of their homes. Turned inward, Cancer can be moodily dependent, emotionally manipulative, and unpredictable. Just as you have figured out the crab, a Cancer will do something different and knock your assumptions on their end. Underneath the shell there is often something very different.

The Water Mother is a very subtle mother, with an outer shell and an inside that is not immediately observable. She will cook for you and clean for you. She will protect you from your enemies and your friends. You may be able to predict her every move, but you may not ever know her soft inner self. You will need to ask. Hera is an excellent example of the Water Mother. She is fiercely protective of her home and even though her husband is a philandering wanderer, she protects her marriage to him. From our end of the twentieth-century perspective, we say she should take it up with him directly and not punish his innocent offspring. While that makes perfect sense, we have no idea what is going on underneath that shell. The Water Mother will respond to questions of the heart and speak from the heart. But you have to ask.

The Mother in Cancer is very emotional and the sign of Cancer explores our emotions in depth. You begin feeling emotions in the watery depths of the womb, nestled close to the heart of your mother. We all know about emotion because we have all experienced happiness, joy, anger, fear, love, hate, and disappointment. Our training in how we handle our emotions begins as soon as we are born.

We may be someone who feels and expresses every thought and emotion as it happens. Or, we may be someone who experiences emotions internally before expressing them. The first is an extroverted response to emotion and the second is an introverted response. Neither is better than the other. Both are merely the way humans respond to emotional data.

Taken to extremes, the emotional Water Mother is truly a Dark Mother. Extroverts can be accused of emotional diarrhea. They pour out every emotion, regardless of how it affects others. The need for revenge is indulged in magnificent ways and love is a grand heightened affair. The ups and downs are enormous. Since there is no regard for others in this grand exuberance of emotion, the extroverted Cancer may find loneliness a bitter pill.

Introverts stuff their emotions and refuse to feel them. The further down they are stuffed, the better it is. "I do not care how tough it is," they say, "it will not bother me." I was a great emotional stuffer. I did a fabulous job. My emotions were not stuffed so much as they were compacted into a tiny, tiny bundle. I stuffed them because that was how I thought it was supposed to be done and because I did not know what to do with all the emotions that I had. Emotions are messy and cause a lot of trouble. A few times over the years, those tiny little bundles exploded on me and created a huge mess, much worse than if I had dealt with them as they happened. I am still introverted, but rather than stuff my emotions I try to experience them and then deal with the situation as it is.

It is good to be smart about your emotions. If you understand yourself, your strengths and weaknesses, then you function better in the world. It is good to know what you have as a shell and what you protect underneath. Then you can decide if this is an emotionally healthy situation or if you need to change.

While the sun is in Cancer, pagans celebrate the festival of Midsummer, the Summer Solstice. This is the longest day of the year, and the shortest night. The Sun God is at his brightest and warmest and the Goddess is at her most fecund, pregnant and growing. The summer is in full force with the fields and meadows full of fruits, vegetables, and flowers, all growing toward harvest. It is exuberant and hopeful. We do not notice that the days will be shortening now. Summer no longer stretches before us in glorious promise. We are well on the path toward harvest. Some things will bear fruit and some things will not, based on our decisions between Beltane and Solstice. We know this underneath the surface, but we celebrate the joy of the moment. This holiday celebrates the outer sun and growth as we dance around the Wheel of the Year.

♋ Shelling Crabs
A Ritual for the Dark Moon in Cancer

Creating Sacred Space: Think about crabs—what they look like and what you know about them. Think of yourself as a crab. What is your shell like, particularly what emotions are on the surface? What is inside, in the soft vulnerable white part? Why is it arranged this way? Does this arrangement satisfy you? Does it work? What, if anything, would you change? Does this help or hinder you?

Cast the Circle: If possible, use water to cast the circle, either from a bowl or spray bottle. Scent it with some lemon or an essential oil. Circle three times, each time doing something different. Skip or dance or hum or whistle or chant. What you do with the water is up to you. You can carry it, spritz it, or sprinkle it. "A circle is cast."

Summon the Guardians and the Elementals:

Summon the West:

> Sunset Guardians of the West, keepers of our emotions, join me in my rite. Sylphs, water creatures of this world, join your power with mine in this rite.

Summon the North:

> Midnight Guardians of the North, bring silence to my rite. Gnomes of the North, silent in the ground, join your power with mine in this rite.

Summon the East:

> Dawn Guardians of the East, join me in my rite. Sylphs, flying into my mind, join your power with mine in my rite.

Summon the South:

> Guardians of noon and of the fiery South, join me in my rite. Bright Salamanders of the broad daylight, join your power with mine in this rite.

Evoke the Goddess:

> Beautiful and loving Hera, Queen of the Gods, Goddess of the Hearth, strong-willed and passionate mother, join me in my sacred circle.

Evoke the God:

> Mighty Poseidon, God of the Sea, protector of the sea creatures and those that crawl on the bottom of the ocean, join me in my sacred circle.

Center and Ground: Envision yourself standing at the edge of the seashore. You are a sturdy blade of beach grass, which survives hurricanes, tornadoes, tidal waves, the harsh drought of summer, and the deep cold of winter. See your roots move downward into the sand at the edge of a salty pool. Your roots move downward through the sand into the bedrock below. Twist a root around a rock as an anchor. Feel the watery energy of the sea mother move up your roots into your body. See your body of grass lifting up toward the sky and smell the salty tang of the water. Feel the energy of the Universe move down to meet you and merge with you. You are grounded in the mother and connected to All That Is.

Statement of Ritual Intent:

> We are beings of emotion, both tender and strong.
> We use them well and we use them badly. They are
> there so we can experience the fullness of life, both
> the bitter and the sweet. As the dark defines the
> light, our bitter emotions define the sweet. The
> surface defines the submerged and the submerged
> defines the surface.

℘ Meditation

You are beside a tidal pool on a warm midsummer beach.
You are surrounded by beach grass and if you look hard
enough you see your grounded self among the grasses.
You are saved. Back beside the pool, you realize that
you are a crab, walking by the edge of the water. Notice
everything you can about your crab body. Notice the
hardness of your shell, the large, hard sharp front claws,
the strong legs, and the weak secondary legs. Because you
are a magical crab, you will see what your shell represents
to you and how it helps you and how it hinders you. Now
look inside. Because you are a magical crab you can see
inside yourself. See the soft white meat and the hard
crunchy bones. Feel the softness. See what parts of you

*are in the soft whiteness and what helps you and what
hinders you. As you center your awareness into your
crab wholeness, see another crab approach you, to teach
you. Ask the other crab to tell you what it sees about you
and your crab-ness. Listen. When it is time, look down
at your pincers and see a gift for your crab teacher. Give
the gift. Your crab teacher will give you a gift. Take it.
When it is time, say goodbye to the crab teacher, and
walk back beside the water. Breathe two times and then
on the third breath, open your eyes, back in the here-and-
now in your human body.*

Raise the Cone of Power: Walk like a crab, that is sideways, around the circle. Dance and sing like a crab around the circle. Celebrate your crabbiness as a positive energy for change. Feel the energy flow through you and around you. When you cannot contain it any longer, send the crabby energy out into the energy with a crescendo of sound.

Cakes and Ale: Take a minute to say a prayer of thanksgiving for the sea creatures, particularly the ones on the bottom. (When I set up my altar, I use Old Bay Seasoning™ as salt—I was born in Baltimore where it is made.)

Center and Ground: See yourself as the beach grass again. Feel the energy of the earth and sky and the tang of salt in the air. Gently loosen your anchoring root and bring it back into yourself. Gently detach your energy from the Universe and pull yourself back. Keep what energy you need and send any excess back to the earth. Move your weight back and forth between your right and left foot. Feel again your closeness to the here and now.

Dismiss the Guardians and the Elementals:

Dismiss the South:

Creatures of fire and of passion, Guardians of our will
and passion, thank you for your presence in my

sacred rite. Go with my thanks and my blessings. Hail and farewell.

Dismiss the West:

Swimmers of the Dark and Guardians of our heart and our joy, thank you for your presence in my sacred rite. Go with my thanks and my blessings. Hail and farewell.

Dismiss the North:

Diggers of Silence and Guardians of the Death and Dark, thank your for your presence in my sacred rite. Go with my thanks and my blessings. Hail and farewell.

Dismiss the East:

Flying ones and Guardians of the air, thank you for your presence in my sacred rite. Go with my thanks and my blessings. Hail and farewell.

Dismiss the Goddess:

Majestic Hera, guardian of our domestic hearts, thank you for your passion and assistance in my sacred circle. Go with my heartfelt thanks. Hail and farewell.

Dismiss the God:

Mighty Poseidon, guardian of the largest creatures and the smallest, thank you for your protection and assistance in my sacred circle. Go with my heartfelt thanks. Hail and farewell.

Open the Circle: Carry the water vessel you used to cast the circle, walk widdershins around the circle. The circle is open but unbroken. Blessed be.

CR

Dark Moon in Leo

The fire sign of Leo is a step of risk on the Dark Moon Path. The spark has become a flame for the Fire Mother and will become wildfire in Sagittarius.

Leo, the lion, is a powerful symbol of creativity and intense activity. The goddesses of several cultures are depicted with lions. Cybele is most often shown riding a lion or accompanied by lions. Artemis is often shown holding lions by their paws. In Crete, adoring lions are companions to the goddess. Hercules conquered the Nemean lion and then wore its skin as his emblem, symbolically donning the lion's intensity and power.

The most powerful of the leonine goddesses is the Egyptian goddess, Sekmet, who is depicted with the head of a lioness and the body of a woman. She represents the fire, flame, and destructive force of the sun. Her name means "Mighty One," and she is the goddess of war. She is a relentless adversary, spreading terror everywhere and all enemies succumb to her onslaughts. Another of her names is Nesert, meaning "flames," and the hot desert winds are her breath. One day she became enraged at the human race and went on a killing spree. Ra mixed a batch of beer and pomegranate juice and left it in her path. Mistaking it for human blood, she drank deeply, became intoxicated, and laid down to sleep it off. After she awoke, her rage was gone. She was also known as the one "great with magic." Her knowledge of sorcery brought her into the service of healing. Like fire, she is a combination of destruction and creation.

Sekmet rampaged through my life during the first year I worked on *Sisters of the Dark Moon*. As I was writing the ritual you will find at the end of this section, I decided to evoke Sekmet. I was concerned since she is such a powerful goddess with a destructive side to her. I decided to go ahead with it, thinking this was not a beginning course in Wicca and, after all, it is not all "tra la la, we all love the Goddess." With a little prayer for the good of all, I wrote the ritual. Less than two weeks before the sun was in Leo that year, the man with whom I had a long and complicated relationship died suddenly while on vacation. He died at the happiest moment of his life. He had just completed a 100-mile endurance run through the mountains in Colorado, achieving a personal record for successful completion. He was forty-four.

While Sekmet rampaged through my life that summer, I was initiated into the great mystery with all its powerful sadness and joy. I learned a lot from him and I loved him very much, even though he was often hard to like. He was hated by many who knew him, but loved by his running companions. I stood in the middle of this powerful dichotomy, seeing both sides of his nature. Those who thought I should not love him and those who thought I should have loved him more sometimes judged me harshly. I learned about forgiveness and more about anger. I learned about peace and I learned about loneliness. I learned about the unexpected support of others and I learned about disappointment when others let me down. I learned about shock and I learned about being in the moment. He had often talked about dying young, about not living beyond his body's ability to run and about not wanting to live without me, so it seemed to me that on some level he chose to die. There was nothing more for him to accomplish. It is all mystery, and there is so much more to say and there is nothing more to say.

In the Tarot, the eighth card of the Major Arcana is Strength. Strength is usually depicted as a lion accompanied by a woman who has her arm around the beast. The woman is dressed in white and has a circlet of flowers in her hair. The obvious translated meaning is "strength." I also interpret the card as harmony with nature and the devas which are nature spirits usually associated with a particular plant. This is not the harmony of lion taming, the circus act of using a whip and a chair. It is the harmony of agreement. That agreement is to live together in respect for each other's nature. It is not cutesy, cuddly lions and sweet-faced humans. It is nature and the harmony of living according to your own nature. It is scary to live in harmony with lions and to respect our own human nature.

The sign of Leo is one of leadership, coupled with acclaim and charisma. Turned inward, Leos are egocentric, overbearing, and concerned with the trappings of fame.

Leo, like all fire signs, is a risk taker. To risk is to dare. To dare is to do something unapproved by others and to accept the consequences, good or bad. To dare to push ourselves to the limit and beyond. To dare is to be the best person we can possibly be by following our own inner passion and our own inner bliss.

These sound like platitudes—bumper stickers and advertisements. They are used that way because these words speak a truth and are scary. To dare is to risk loss. To dare is to risk disapproval and loss of love. It is an enormous undertaking and one that takes great creativity. The energy of Leo brings great drama and great comedy to risk. You need both.

The Fire Mother is daring and an inspiration to her children. She burns with a brilliant flame that draws everyone to her circle. She is creative, witty, and filled with laugher. People enjoy being around her most of the time. Her flame does singe. Flying around her flame means that people get caught in the flame and catch fire. The flame casts a shadow that flickers in and out and is hard to see. We often see it out of the corner of our eyes. Despite her bright flame, the Fire Mother moves subtly in the shadow world. The shadow may contain the secret to her soul. The Fire Mother does things, she says, for our "own good." Sometimes she does things for a reason we may not readily perceive.

The Fire Mother wants us to risk and the Fire Mother wants us to be happy. She knows, probably, that we cannot always do both. A television commercial from the 1970s shows this contradiction. In the middle of a professional football game, a matronly woman runs onto the field, yelling "yoo-hoo" to her son. So all the huge burly men stop playing this rough, violent sport to pay attention to this comparatively small mother. She finds her son and exhorts him to eat his cereal. After mowing down all the football players' objections and getting them to promise to eat their cereal, she departs with the advice, "Play nice, but win."

We all know that playing nice is not about playing to win. Yet our Fire Mother wants us to do both. Or does she want us to examine our ethics and re-examine what it means to win? We must rely on our creativity and ability to think outside what is considered the norm in order to live an expansive, transformed life. It is a risk. We risk not winning, we risk being laughed at, we risk not being loved and we risk not being nice. If we do not take a risk, we risk being mediocre, being unhappy, and we risk not being part of the mystery.

ଔ To Dare the Great Mystery
A Ritual for the Dark Moon in Leo

Creating Sacred Space: Spend some time thinking about what scares you and what you risk to do the thing that scares you. What do you gamble when you take a risk? What do you keep when you do not take a risk? In preparation, risk something. Do not do the *biggest* thing you can think of; do a symbolic thing. If you are concerned about money or have never gambled, buy a lottery ticket. If you are ashamed of your body, wear shorts to the grocery store. Ask yourself, what is holding me back from the Mystery? You will be evoking some powerful deities in this ritual, so be careful and respectful. You are strong enough and have enough experience. It is the risk.

Cast the Circle: With a candle or other flame symbol, walk deosil around the circle three times, chanting, "A circle is cast."

Summon the Guardians and Elementals of the Directions:

Summon the South:

> Dark Amazons and Warriors of the South, you who
> burn with the bright light and dark shadow, bring us
> your passion, fire, and daring. Salamanders, bright
> flaming ones of the South, join me in my sacred
> circle. Hail and welcome.

Summon the West:

> Dark Mothers and Lovers of the West, you who
> flow into the Dark and the Light, bring to us your
> emotion, tears, and love. Undines, watery ones of the
> West, join me in my sacred circle. Hail and welcome.

Summon the North:

> Dark Crones and Sages of the North, you ground
> with your stability and wisdom, bring us your
> patience, wisdom, and serenity. Gnomes, earth ones
> of the North, join me in my sacred circle. Hail and
> welcome.

Summon the East:

> Dark Maidens and Youths of the East, you who
> breathe the breath of intellect, newness, and vitality,
> bring us your intelligence, freshness, and youth.
> Sylphs, airy ones of the East, join me in my sacred
> circle. Hail and welcome.

Center and Ground: You are standing in an oasis in the middle of the desert, vast and hot. You are the moss surrounding the oasis pool. Feel the moist soil beneath you as you cast your roots downward and outward. You go down and outward in all directions, weaving a tapestry of roots connecting with the sandy heart of the mother. You are rooted, firm in the Desert Mother. Cast your consciousness upward toward the heated sky. Feel the hot embrace of Father Sky reach down and connect with you. You are connected in the embrace of the Father and rooted in the love of the Mother.

Statement of Ritual Intent:

> We are creatures of our society and of our upbringing.
> What we think is true is often a product of what we
> have experienced and it is not a universal truth. As
> we realize our "place" in society, we develop ways to
> fit in, even if it is not in our own best interest. We
> are tied to our social upbringing but sometimes we
> need to break away and be something different. It is a
> risk to dare to do that. We often experience anger at
> the unfairness of life. We cannot always have it both

ways—to be accepted and to be our selves. I am a
lion. We will meditate on the lion and then we will
roar!

☪ Meditation

*You are standing in the heat of an African savannah. It is
hot and the air is filled with the sounds and smells of myr-
iad creatures. They are exotic to you at first, and then
you realize, gradually, that they seem familiar to you, as
if you have been there all of your life. You look down at
your hands and feet and see that they are the gigantic
paws of a lion. You are aware of your tail and your skin
and your mane, if you have one. You know that you are
a member of a strong pride and you work together, hunt-
ing and raising children. You walk off from the pride and
go on a journey. You pass through many landscapes and
see many things. Some things are important for you to
know. Remember them. You come to the edge of a river
and there stands Sekmet, that fearsome goddess, the Eye
of Ra and she who sees all. She sees straight into the heart
of you. Stand and wait for her to speak to you. She will
tell you what is enraging you, what is stopping you. She
will tell you what you have to risk. The third thing she
will tell you will be like the draught of pomegranate juice;
this is what will soothe you. Remember these things.
When the time is right, you will notice in your right paw a
gift for Sekmet. Give it to her. Ask her if there is a gift or
any last words for you. Listen. Retrace your steps. You
are back with your pride. Romp a little. When the time
is right, look down at your paws and find that they are
hands and feet again. Breathe two times. Then on your
third breath, open your eyes and find yourself back in
your magic, sacred circle.*

Raise the Cone of Power: Start by walking like a lion around the circle. Shake your head or mane, swish your tail. Know that you have a powerful body and powerful persona. Start to roar, softly at first. Louder, louder. Roar Roar Roar. ROAR ROAR ROAR ROAR. You are lion! Feel the energy blast into the universe.

Cakes and Ale: Say a prayer of thanksgiving and rip into the food and drink with roaring gusto.

Center and Ground: You are beside the oasis, the moss heated by the hot sun. Cast your awareness to your roots. Pull them back from all directions and up from the depths of the sand. Know that you can always connect with the Mother. Cast your awareness upward and to the embrace with Father Sky. Gently release the embrace, knowing that you can always return to the love of all-that-is. You are back in your circle. Centered and grounded in the love of the Universe.

Dismiss the Guardians and the Elementals:

Dismiss the East:

> Creatures of the air, flying through the heat of day
> and Guardians of the mind, thank you for your
> presence in my sacred rite. Go with my thanks and
> my blessings. Hail and farewell.

Dismiss the South:

> Creatures of the heat and the fire and Guardians of
> the hot, hot sunlit day, thank you for your presence
> in my sacred rite. Go with my thanks and my
> blessings. Hail and farewell.

Dismiss the West:

> Creatures of the ponds and puddles and Guardians of
> the power of emotion, thank you for your presence in
> my sacred rite. Go with my thanks and my blessings.
> Hail and farewell.

Dismiss the North:

> Creatures of hot darkness and Guardians of the Final
> Silence, thank you for your presence in my sacred
> rite. Go with my thanks and my blessings. Hail and
> farewell.

Dismiss the Goddess:

> Great and honest Sekmet, thank you for what you
> have shown me. Go with my love, thanks, and
> respect. Bright blessings. Fare thee well.

Dismiss the God:

> Glorious Ra, the father of our daylight hours, thank
> you for what you have shown me. Go with my love,
> thanks and respect. Bright Blessings. Fare thee well.

Open the Circle: With the candle or flame symbol, go three
times widdershins around the circle. The circle is open, but
unbroken.

ℰℐ

Dark Moon in Virgo

The Dark Moon Path takes a deeper step into Virgo, an earth sign. The soil becomes a mountain in Virgo and will shake into an earthquake in Capricorn.

Virgo is the sign of the virgin goddess who is not an indication of sexual chastity but rather self-possession, a sense that the woman is heart-whole. Virgo is also the time of great harvest and the celebration of the end of the agricultural year. So if Virgo is the sign of the virgin goddess, why is it designated as the sign of the Earth Mother on this Dark Moon Path? Complexity. During the moon in Virgo we find a celebration of the Goddess in her maiden, mother, and crone aspect. The Earth Mother, Demeter, mourning the loss of her maiden daughter, Persephone, plunges the Earth into winter, causing the leaves to fall and the temperature to drop. We see the beginning of the Crone. All three aspects of the goddess show in the Earth Mother story. The Earth Mother has a vision and perspective that transcends time and space. Through the Earth Mother we can see where we have been, where we are, and where we are going. Through the Earth Mother we see the endless cycle of the wheel of the year.

Virgo is a complex sign with very strong characteristics. Virgo is very practical, fastidious about details, economical, and highly organized. Turned inward, Virgos are obsessive, critical, and probably cannot see the forest for the trees. Imagine a mother raising children alone. She may feel that she has to be organized, dutiful, and economical, while her children, not understanding the complexity of the situation, may feel she is critical, faultfinding, and judgmental.

The Earth Mother is a symbol present in our modern consciousness. Sometimes fat women are called Earth Mothers in a supposedly kind euphemism designed to excuse their fatness. On a more positive note, the Earth Mother is our vision of fecundity and nurturing motherhood. On a darker side, the Earth Mother is the mother of the harvest where we must die a little to be reborn. When I was growing up in Maryland, we were still harvesting vegetables in late August to late September, something that does not happen in upstate New York where I now live. When I was in junior high, we canned tomatoes and peppers, made jelly, pickled cucumbers and watermelon rind so that we supplemented our cupboard for the winter. By late August and early September, I was heartily sick of the whole hot, sticky process. I remember thinking, in the midst of the smell of rotting vegetables, that there was too much fecundity. I had just learned that word and it seemed a neat turn of phrase. So much for an Earth Mother in training! I can just imagine what my mother and grandmother felt. Here again, we have the Maiden, Mother, and Crone.

While the sun is in Virgo, pagans celebrate the fall equinox, Mabon. Like the spring equinox, it is the time when the day and night are equal in length. After Mabon, the nights become progressively longer and the days become shorter. It is a time to reflect on balance and temperance, knowing that moderation is a key concept for living. In the spring we reflect on growth and the excitement of new life. In the fall the leaves are falling and the temperatures are dropping. All of life is preparing for winter. Birds start flying south and squirrels start gathering nuts. The plants become part of the earth again. Trees are preparing for winter by dropping their leaves and pooling their sap. We balance the fall equinox with the spring, seeing balance as the whole year in perspective: spring as life and fall as death, and back to spring again in the endless turning of the Wheel of the Year.

Sometimes balance has a longer range than what we may see in front of us. This is commonly called "the big picture." To completely dedicate oneself to the preparation for dying may not seem balanced, however in the overall picture of the year, it has great symmetry. Sometimes when we see a person who we think is out of balance or unbalanced, there may be a perspective that we do not see.

The quality associated with Virgo is silence. It is part of the sayings in Wicca associated with the four directions. In the east, it is "to know," in the south, "to will." In the west, it is "to dare," and in the north, "to be silent." *To be silent is not to be silenced.* To be silent is to choose to be silent. That is a powerful choice.

Often, little girls are taught to listen and not to talk, to be good and to be quiet, and not to put themselves forward in any pushy way. In classrooms, boys are called on first and are often rewarded for interrupting while girls are called on last and are often punished for calling out answers or interrupting. This has a chilling effect on girls as students, and they often feel silenced. A lot of feminist discourse on classroom behavior, male-female communication, and women's behavior is concerned with this silencing. It is so inculcated in women's behavior that they may not call out in a situation when they need to or when their lives are in danger.

One of the outgrowths of the feminist movement are self-defense courses such as FIGHTBACK or Model Mugging which teaches women to scream and yell and to fight back against their attackers, to call out for their own safety. Even women who have taken kung fu and other martial arts still have difficulty calling out when they are attacked. It is a difficult lesson to learn, particularly for women who were raised to be quiet, good girls. When they finally learn to scream, yell, and fight back, it is a transforming experience.

So what does it mean to be silent as an assertion of our will and our power? How can we use silence for good and not to harm others? Misapplied, silence can be a sullen punishment, designed to manipulate others' behavior. Silence, appropriately applied in an atmosphere of love and trust, can be a powerful instrument of self-discovery. Frequently, if you are comfortable in silence, you can make important discoveries. Therapists often let there be silence in a session. The client, rushing to fill the void of silence, may say things they may not have intended and may reveal important thoughts, attitudes, or information.

A few years ago, I supervised a graduate intern. We had bi-weekly sessions where we discussed her work and her plans. It was very stimulating for me since I had been out of graduate school for a long time. I was learning a lot. Toward the end of the term, she made a comment that I was so quiet that she felt like she had to rush in and just say something. Because of that, she indicated, she said more than she had intended and learned more than she thought possible. I was not doing it on purpose. I was just waiting to see if there was more to be said. I learned a lot too.

If we are comfortable in silence, we may find the wisdom of our own minds will speak to us. Since we live in a world filled with sound, being comfortable with silence is a hard lesson to learn. We are inundated with sound from the television, from radio, and from cars. The television is on "just for company," we say. What if we fill the house with silence, just for company? What does your home sound like without talking, without television or radio? What goes on inside your head? It is not silent by any means. The clocks tick, the refrigerator runs, and you hear all sorts of things. Sometimes you hear the voice of the Goddess.

I used to be uncomfortable with silence. I always turned on the television or the radio for company. I would get into the car and would not be able to drive a mile without having the radio on or a tape playing. I would go to sleep with the radio playing. Some of that is a function of living alone in a busy suburb where there was a lot of noise from traffic, sirens, and people, so I blocked out the noise of traffic and other activities by playing the radio or having the television on. Later, for four years, I lived with a man who did not like a lot of noise, so he would turn down the radio or turn off the television so things would be quiet. I learned to deal with silence and then to be comfortable with it. Gradually I realized that I had learned to embrace silence. So when the radio broke in my car and I did not really want to spend the money to fix it, I found it was no big deal to be without a radio, even on long drives. I had my own inner voice and the voice of the Goddess for company. Before it would have been a major tragedy. After two years, I got the radio fixed as a treat to myself. I felt two emotions. I did not miss much when it came to popular music and I felt like it was an enormous gift to have music back again.

Now, I walk every day on the trails with the dogs. I do not take a radio. I watch and listen. I hear birds, frogs, and water flowing in the creek. I hear trees creak in the wind. There is a lot to see and hear. Sometimes I hear the voice inside my head.

I hear the spirits speak to me and the clear voice of the Goddess.

Silence is valuable. Knowing when to speak and when to listen is a valuable skill. To be still and quiet while others search their heart and soul is an action of love and honor. Listening is an active part of the conversation. To still your own inner voice to hear what people have to say is an act of love and compassion. You can do this when you embrace your own silence.

∞ To Own the Silence
A Ritual for the Dark Moon in Virgo

Creating Sacred Space: Spend some time noticing how much noise is in your life. Do you turn on the radio or television, just for company? That is neither right nor wrong, it just is. Do you avoid silences? Can you drive a distance without the radio? Spend some time in silence. How do you feel about silence? What is it like? You will need a bowl with some soil in it for the meditation.

Cast the Circle: Without speaking, chanting, or singing, walk clockwise around the circle, three times.

Summon the Guardians and Elementals:

Summon the North:

> Silent Guardians of the North, silent speakers of
> wisdom of the earth, join me in my sacred circle.
> Gnomes, creatures of the earth and stone, join me
> in my sacred circle. Hail and welcome.

Summon the East:

> Guardians of the East, wise ones of the mind, join
> me in my sacred circle. Sylphs, creatures of the air
> and wind, join me in my sacred circle. Hail and
> welcome.

Dismiss the South:

Passionate Guardians of the South, speakers of will
and desire, join me in my sacred circle. Salamanders,
creatures of fire and flame, join me in my sacred
circle. Hail and welcome.

Dismiss the West:

Water Guardians of the West, loving speakers of the
heart, join me in my sacred circle. Undines, creatures
of the sea and beaches, join me in my sacred circle.
Hail and welcome.

Evoke the Goddess:

Mother Demeter, earth goddess with the power to
silence the growth of the world, join me in my rite.
Bring with you the strength of powerful emotion and
the wisdom of the earth. Hail and welcome.

Evoke the God:

Mighty and fearsome Hades, lord of the final silence,
death, join me in my rite. Bring with you the vision
of all of life and death and the wisdom of the final
transformation.

Center and Ground: You are a very old rock, firmly planted
deep in the earth. Cast your awareness downward and feel the
comfort and embrace of the earth as you experience the solid
ground around you and beneath you. Cast your awareness to the
surface of the rock and feel the heat of the sun warm you throughout. Stay there for a moment and feel the warmth of the sun and
the comfort of the earth. You are centered and grounded in the
Love of the Universe.

Statement of Ritual Intent:

Silence is a wonderful gift and one that we are not
always comfortable with. Silence is not the absence

of sound, but the presence of listening with my heart as well as my mind. This journey is to go to the heart of silence.

Ritual Work: This is a silent meditation. Keep a low light or a candle to light the room slightly. Take the bowl of soil and stare into it until you see only the dirt and let the silence of Mother Earth speak to you.

Raise the Cone of Power: You will need to be tuned into what the Dark Mother wants you to do! Rise up and dance around the circle. If your meditation leads you to sing, dance, clap, and chant, do so. Otherwise, dance around the circle in attentive silence, feeling the power well up inside you and WHOOSH into the Universe.

Cakes and Ale: Say a prayer of thanks for the Earth and her wisdom. Say thank you to the Mother for the wisdom of when to speak and when to be silent.

Center and Ground: You are the rock, firmly seated in the earth and warmed through by the sun. Stay for a moment and feel the warmth, love, and power. Slowly bring yourself back into your human body, grounded and centered in the love of the Universe.

Release the Guardians and the Elementals:

Dismiss the West:

> Loving creatures of the sand and beach and
> Guardians of our Heart, thank you for your presence
> in my sacred rite. Go with my thanks and my
> blessings. Hail and farewell.

Dismiss the South:

> Passionate creatures of the heated lands, and
> Guardians of the Will, thank you for your presence
> in my sacred rite. Go with my thanks and my
> blessings. Hail and welcome.

Dismiss the East:

Creatures of clear vision and Guardians of Thought, thank you for your presence in my sacred rite. Go with my thanks and my blessings. Hail and farewell.

Dismiss the North:

Silent creatures of the rock and soil and Guardians of the Dark Silence, thank you for your presence in my sacred rite. Go with my thanks and my blessings. Hail and farewell.

Release the God:

Awesome and Mighty Hades, the Guardian of the Dead and Lord of the Dark Silence, thank you for the power of your presence. Go with my thanks and my blessings. Hail and farewell.

Release the Goddess:

Mother Demeter, Lady of the Seasons, thank you for your presence in my sacred rite. Go with my thanks and my blessings. Hail and farewell.

Open the Circle in silence.

CR

The Mystery of the Mother

The Goddess as Mother moves away from the "doings" of the Maiden into a world filled with others. The Air Mother, the Water Mother, the Fire Mother, and the Earth Mother are part of the whole picture of the Mother Goddess, yet there is always a mystery about the Mother. You think you know her as she nurtures us, scolds us, holds us to high standards, and loves us. Yet do we? We often see the Mother as part of ourselves, yet it seems there is a part of her that is secret and separate from ourselves. It is her own personal attachment and connection to the part of the Universe that creates. Each of us connects into the creation energy in unique and special ways. The Mother gives us examples and guides us to our own connection, but in the end, all of us find our own special connection to Creation. And that is part of the mystery of the Mother, by "being" she helps us to become human Be-INGS.

We become defined by who we are and not by what we do.

❧

The Dark Crone

The Dark Crone

The Dark Moon Path descends to unbelievable depths as we approach the Goddess as Crone. We see the season of winter as the season of the Crone. The leaves fall from the trees and show us a stark vision of the world that is cold and seems deserted. We have to look to see the beauty and we have to search to find the joy.

The word "crone" evokes strong emotions in us. We see images of fearsome old women with no teeth and wrinkles that never seem to end. Crone evokes images of a witch burning Hansel and Gretel in an oven. Crone evokes images of dark, stormy nights filled with terror and screams. Crone looks into the heart and tells us of magic and a mystery that is full of awe and wonder if we are brave and look into the abyss. We must look beyond the fearsome displays of power and might. The modern feminist movement and the women's spirituality movement has worked to reclaim the word crone as one of power and magic.

Crones were regarded as powerful because they did not bleed. They had strong magic to hold back the flow of monthly menses and keep the power of blood within. Wicca celebrates the Waning Moon as the moon of the Crone. She is so strong that she can hold back the light of the moon.

We approach the Crone, seeking her wisdom and acknowledging her power. The Crone has earned her right to be powerful through living her life to the fullest. She knows of sorrow, pain, and joy. She knows of choices made. These choices may be good ones and bad ones. She knows that the important thing is to make the choice. The Crone never says, "I have no choice." She says, "I choose."

Crones are active and moving. Crones work alone and they work with others. After all, that is what cronies are. Crones do not sit on a cliff, granting audiences to supplicants. Crones demand. Crones act. Crones create, move, sing, talk, kvetch, dance, walk, run, and more. It is action and purpose that characterizes the Crone. Action and purpose.

The Crone goddesses are often fearsome, women who hold life and death in their hands. The Fates pursue heroes and harry them to their destiny. Threesomes weave the thread of life, and then cut it off. Cerridwen stirs the cauldron of life and death. Hecate challenges us to life and to death.

It is easy to see the Dark in the Crone. She has seen life and she has seen death. She knows that life is cut short or life goes on too long. She knows that death comes quickly with incredible shock. She knows that death teases us with disease, illness, and lingering pain. She knows that life comes with puppies and babies. She knows that life comes when an elderly woman takes a poetry class for the first time and spends her last years writing the poetry she kept inside during her youth. The Dark and the Crone naturally weave together because she sees the irony and the blessing as joy interweaves with grief. The Crone knows that with the bitter comes the sweet. The Crone knows and understands.

CR

Dark Moon in Libra

We begin the journey of the Crone with the air sign of
Libra. Air was a breath in Aquarius and wind in Gemini
and a storm in Libra. The Crone acts on balance and
intellect in Libra.

Libra is symbolized as balanced scales, showing us justice. In the United States, the scales are held by a blind-
folded Justice, evoking an impartial and fair balance of
punishment and reward that is our system of courts. It is
an ideal that we fear that we have never obtained and
we fear that we have perverted justice beyond redemp-
tion. In ancient Egyptian culture, Libra occurred in the
month when the harvest was weighed before selling or
storing it. It was a time of measuring success or failure.
The Egyptian goddess Ma'at was the guardian of justice

89

and she measured the human soul on a scale balanced with an ostrich feather. I believe that the scales of Libra balance justice and forgiveness. In life we get what we deserve and that is justice. What we deserve is joy and that is forgiveness.

My experience of Librans is not of balance, at least not a balance that we can see from a close perspective. Some Librans I have known were really extreme personalities. What I learned from them is that being balanced is not about being even-tempered, calm, or temperate. Balance is looking at the whole picture from a long perspective and about looking at all sides. Do you remember science or chemistry classes where you had to measure and balance things? You usually started at one end of the spectrum and then added or subtracted another sub-stance until you achieved a balanced reading. When did you ever start out balanced? As we have learned from the two equi-nox sabbats, balance is often part of a picture that is larger than we perceive.

Libra is also about judgment: good judgment and bad; weigh-ing and measuring; active and moving, Libra works with both success and failure. Libras seek the balance of harmony and truth. Turned inward, Libras are out of control, vain, and dependent.

The time of the Crone is the time of action. The Air Crone uses her mind and the world of facts to balance and weigh events. She has the power to move and to change not only herself but also the world around her. She cuts through our small attempts to appear capable and successful to tell the truth. Sometimes being on the receiving end of those observations is difficult. The Air Crone blows into our life like a whirlwind and gets to the heart of the matter. If in getting to the heart of the situation, the Air Crone speaks from her heart, we will find our way to joy. The Air Crone knows the secrets of life and death. She knows that the mind can change the world and that the heart and mind together can transform the world. Combining the heart and mind together, the Air Crone knows the Dark.

The Air Crone blows into Libra as a storm. When this chapter was first written there had been some devastating hurricanes in the southern United States. Since I spent most of my life in hurricane country, I know what it is like living with the threat of hurricanes. My family tells hurricane stories, about crossing the then new Chesapeake Bay bridge soon after it was built, in the middle of a storm that threatened to turn into a hurricane, and other stories. Hurricanes destroy houses and other buildings, and kill people. Yet, ABC News broadcasted a report on the benefits of hurricanes. Hurricanes, particularly those out in the ocean, keep the temperature balanced across the globe, preventing global extremes in temperature. When hurricanes come into land, they create new land masses, dredging out bays and streams. Hurricanes also blow in new plants, animals, and birds. This stormy action revitalizes the land and the ecosystem, preventing the area affected from being depleted of nutrients needed for a robust ecology. It is only when puny human dwellings get in the way that we call hurricanes destructive. It is an astonishing perspective on a natural "disaster."

The Air Crone brings us to descent. At the beginning of this journey in the air sign of Aquarius, we stood on the abyss and looked in. The Air Crone pushes us into the abyss, challenging us to descend inward. There are descent stories in many of the cultures of the world. While there are men and gods who make the descent, the majority of the stories are about women and goddesses who descend to the Underworld. I believe that the descent journey is the principal female story of myth and magic. Just as men have the heroic journey and the vision quest, women have the descent story.

The descent story tells us that a woman or a goddess loses their dearest loved one, usually a daughter or sister. She descends to the Underworld to retrieve the beloved or to connect with the beloved. In the process of the descent, she is challenged until she loses everything. She faces the final test naked, unadorned, and utterly vulnerable.

The story of Inanna is such a descent story. The Queen of the Heavens, Inanna, is a glorious and beautiful Goddess who is also a new bride. She hears that her sister, Queen of the Underworld, Ereshkigal, has lost her husband. Inanna goes to the Underworld to mourn with her sister. She begins her descent against the advice of her closest advisors and loved ones. She comes to a gate where she is stopped. The custodian of the gate demands her crown and she surrenders it. Inanna goes through seven gates, surrendering all that adorns her and all that she values. When she reaches the throne of her sister, she is naked and vulnerable. In her most terrible aspect, as the Destroyer, Ereshkigal kills Inanna and hangs her on a hook.

Through the efforts of her son, her woman attendant, and a magician, Inanna is rescued from death and regains her finery. She departs dressed in her crown with a promise that she will send another to stay in the Underworld in her place. Upon her return to the heavens, she finds that only her son, woman attendant, and the magician mourned her absence. Her husband and his sister celebrated their elevation to royalty and did not mourn the loss of their beloved. Inanna then sent her husband to the Underworld for six months and his sister to the Underworld for six months, balancing justice with forgiveness.

The ritual that follows is a descent ritual. I had the privilege of being in a descent ritual that we called "The Descent of Anna" (I changed the name in the interest of privacy). Anna is faced with severe health problems and went into a crisis. Through the neglect of health-care practitioners and the complexity of her condition, she nearly died. Her recovery was painful and difficult. Upon recovery from the crisis, she wanted a ritual that would set her back on the path of healing, not only of her body but also of her heart and soul. This is the ritual we did, now adapted for a solitary meditation.

I had the Queen of the Underworld invoked into me so that I could greet Anna after her descent. She went though each gate where precious things were asked or demanded of her. It is harder than you might think, reading this in the light. At the end, she came before the Queen of the Underworld. Anna had given up everything. Yet the Dark Queen saw and took more. In the end, the Queen of the Underworld gathered up everything that was taken away and cast it into a crystal. She handed it back to Anna as a gift, as the Jewel of Herself. Completely unadorned and vulnerable, she was given back the greatest jewel of all, herself.

The meditation accompanying the ritual that follows is designed to take you on that journey. It is a long one, so give yourself ample time. If you are a man doing this ritual, please use the female pronouns when referring to yourself. This ritual speaks to the feminine part of you.

☊ The Descent
A Ritual for the Dark Moon in Libra

Creating Sacred Space: Spend some time thinking about what happened when you looked into the abyss. What did you see? What looked back at you? Think about what is precious to you? What adorns you?

Casting the Circle: Holding a feather or other symbol of air, walk three times deosil around the circle, chanting, "A circle is cast."

Summoning the Guardians and the Elementals:

Summon the East:

> Grandmothers and Grandfathers of the East, bring insight and honesty and join me in my sacred circle. Sylphs of the air and of play, join me in my sacred circle. Hail and welcome.

Summon the South:

> Crones and Sages of the South, bring passion and energy and join me in my sacred circle. Salamanders of the fire and flame, join me in my sacred circle. Hail and welcome.

Summon the West:

> Ancient Ones of the West, bring all emotion and join me in my sacred circle. Undines of the ocean and pond, join me in my sacred circle. Hail and welcome.

Summon the North:

> Aged Ones of the North, bring wisdom and silence and join me in my sacred circle. Gnomes, diggers of the ground and the soul, join me in my sacred circle.

Evoke the Goddess:

> Queen of the Heavens and Queen of the Under-world, she who mourns and she who guards my fears, join me in my sacred circle. Hail and welcome.

Evoke the God:

> Dark Lord of Death, he who guards the darkness of death and guards our terrors, join me in my sacred circle. Hail and welcome.

Center and ground: Take three breaths and close your eyes. See yourself lying on the ground, face up to the sky. Feel the breezes rock you. You are a fallen tree with your roots uprooted and your branched arms flung wide. Time moves swiftly through the seasons and you begin to rot. You melt into the soil and become a part of it. Your backbone sinks deeper into the ground as you become part of the soil and mulch of the ground. The sun, rain, and time move together to bring you into a new connectedness with the earth. You are the earth. You cannot tell where the ground begins and you end. Feel the heartbeat of the Mother as you fall into her embrace. Breathe into your center and be grounded. Open your eyes.

Statement of Ritual Intent:

The descent is an important journey in my life as Goddess. The descent speaks to the female within all humans and in me especially. I descend into the depths of the spiral to discover the Dark, the abyss, and the Jewel that I am.

℞ Meditation

You are standing on the edge of the abyss with the Queen of the Heavens. She embraces you, looks you in the eye, and shoves you into the abyss with a mighty push. You fall downward into the Dark. You land softly at the beginning of a downward path. You walk downward and you come to the First Gate.

The Guardian of the Gate, clothed in a sky-blue pink cloak, stops you and says, "I am the Guardian of the Eastern Gate. Will you give me your beliefs? Will you give me your vision and your notions about life? Will you give me your intellect, your knowledge, and your education?"

You reply to the Guardian and talk as is necessary about the demands. The Guardian opens the Eastern Gate for you and you pass through. You walk farther along the path and you come to the second Gate.

*The Guardian, clothed in a red-yellow-orange cloak,
stops you and says, "I am the Guardian of the Southern
Gate. Give me your expectations, your passion, your
desire, your sexuality, your power, your magic, and your
spells. Give me your will and your accomplishments on
the world."*

*You reply to the Guardian and talk as is necessary about
the demands. The Guardian opens the Southern Gate for
you and you pass through. You walk farther along the
path and you come to the Third Gate.*

*The Guardian, clothed in a blue and green cloak, stops
you and says, "I am the Guardian of the Western Gate.
Give me your loves and your hates, your sensuality, and
your fears. Give me your dreams and your joys. Give me
your emotions."*

*You reply to the Guardian and talk as is necessary about
the demands. The Guardian opens the Western Gate for
you and you pass through. The path is darker now and
steeper. You walk further until you come to the Fourth
Gate.*

*The Guardian, clothed in a brown cloak, says to you, "I
am the Guardian of the Northern Gate. Give me your
silence. Give me your orgasms, your birth, your death,
your health, and your diseases. Give me your cures, your
journeys, your life, your death, and your flesh."*

*You reply to the Guardian and talk as is necessary about
the demands. The Guardian opens the Northern Gate for
you and you pass through. The path is impenetrably dark
and you move blindly forward. You come to the Fifth Gate.*

*The Guardian, who you cannot see, says, "I am the
Guardian of the Gate of Above. I demand your religion,*

your spirits, your guides, and your notions of good and evil. I demand your scriptures, your notions of Light and Dark."

You reply to the Guardian and talk as is necessary about the demands. The Guardian is revealed to you and the Gate is opened for you and you pass through to The Dark Path. You walk farther until you come to the Sixth Gate.

The Guardian, who you cannot see, says, "I am the Guardian of the Gate of Below. I demand your shadow, your history, your notions of good and evil. I demand your injuries and your unknowns. I demand your notions of Light and Dark."

You reply to the Guardian and talk as is necessary about the demands. The Guardian is revealed to you and the Gate is opened for you. You pass through and walk further until you come to the Seventh Gate.

The Guardian, who you cannot see, says, "I am the Guardian of the Spirit Gate. I demand your limitations, your boundaries, your transformations, your successes, and your failures. I demand your lifetimes, your destiny, and your karma."

You reply to the Guardian and talk as is necessary about the demands. You have nothing left as the Guardian is revealed to you. The Gate opens before you and you step into the courtyard of the Queen of the Underworld. Walk forward until you are standing before the Queen of the Underworld. She removes her cloak and you see the glorious Queen in all her Dark Splendor. She looks at you and says, "You have something left and I take it from you. I take everything from you." She rips what is left from the center of your being in a swift, terrible, and

mighty movement of her hand. You are left bereft as you
stand before her with nothing.

The Queen of the Underworld takes you into her Dark
Embrace and holds you. She says, "You are our Beloved
Sister, dearly loved because of all your sadness and all
your joy." She hands you a beautiful jewel. "This is the
Jewel of You. You adorn the World, above and below."

The Queen gives a mighty shout and her voice opens all
the Gates and brings all the Guardians in a circle around
you. "This is our Beloved Sister, Sister of the Dark
Moon. Welcome her to our Sorority." They gather
around you, hugging, kissing, and welcoming you. They
take you back up the path through every Gate until you
are in the presence of the Queen of the Heavens. She
embraces you and looks you in the eye. You look back
and see yourself. Strong women like strong women.
Strong goddesses know strong goddesses when they see
one. You are one. You hear the voice of both Queens
telling you about the Jewel and any other words you need
to hear. Finally they embrace you and say "Goodbye
Sister." Breathe three times. On the third breath, open
your eyes.

Raising the Cone of Power: Move around the circle chanting, "I am the Queen of Light, I am the Queen of Dark. I am the Queen of Light, I am the Queen of Dark." Move and chant until the power rises up and through you into the Universe with a large WHOOSH.

Cakes and Ale:

Thank you, Dark Queen and Light, for the journey today. Thank you for all that I learned and all that I will learn. Thank you for this food and drink that

will help ground this experience into my body and
into the here-and-now. Blessed be.

Center and Ground: Close your eyes and you are the tree
again, connected to the earth. You are the mulch and the soil.
Notice that you begin to separate yourself little by little. You can
feel your backbone as you stretch it and move it a little. You can
feel your toes as you wiggle them a little. You feel your arms and
hands as you move them. You feel your head as you rock it gently
back and forth. Gently feel your connection with the earth
recede a little. You are always part of the Mother and for now
you are back in your self.

Dismiss the God:

> Mighty Lord of the Dark, Master of Compassion,
> thank you for your wisdom and your care. Go from
> my sacred circle with my blessings and my thanks.
> Farewell.

Dismiss the Goddess:

> Queens of Light and Dark, starry Sister Goddesses,
> thank you for your love and your honesty. Go from
> my sacred circle with my thanks and my blessings.
> Farewell.

Dismiss the Guardians and the Elementals:

Dismiss the North:

> Gnomes of the earth and rock, thank you for your
> patience. Go from my sacred circle with my thanks
> and my blessings. Aged Ones of the North, thank
> you for your healing and your insight. Go from my
> sacred circle with my thanks and my blessings.
> Farewell.

Dismiss the West:

Undines, playful mermaids, thank you for your joy.
Go from my sacred circle with my thanks and my
blessings. Ancient ones of the West, thank you for
your heartfelt wisdom. Go from my sacred circle with
my thanks and my blessings. Farewell.

Dismiss the South:

Salamanders, slithering with fire, thank you for your
magic. Go from my sacred circle with my thanks and
my blessings. Sages and Crones of the South, thank
you for the Dance of Life. Go from my sacred circle
with my thanks and my blessings. Farewell.

Dismiss the East:

Airy Sylphs, creatures of the zephyrs, thank you for
thoughts, good and bad. Go from my sacred circle
with my thanks and my blessings. Grandfathers and
Grandmothers of the East, thank you for the vision
and for clarity. Go from my sacred circle with my
thanks and my blessings. Farewell.

Open the Circle: With the feather or air sign, walk three times
widdershins around the circle. The circle is open but unbroken.

☞

Dark Moon in Scorpio

The Dark Moon Path takes a dive into the deep-water world of Scorpio. Water was a drop in Pisces, a stream in Cancer, and swells into a tidal wave in Scorpio. The Crone acts on the heart in Scorpio.

The symbol for Scorpio is the scorpion, a nocturnal arachnid. This scientific identification does not illustrate the profound and disturbing regard in which the scorpion is held in many cultures. In myth and in story, the scorpion is a disturbingly threatening and venomous creature. In Greek myth, Artemis sent the scorpion to kill Orion because of his pride. The scorpion caused the steeds of Apollo to bolt when his son Phaethon tried to steer the solar chariot. The Earth was scorched when Phaethon died. Scorpions were associated with Mars, the God of War. In a 1950s movie, a nuclear explosion created gigantic and monstrous scorpions that were destroyed by the hero while the heroine screamed.

Scorpio is an extremely complex sign, full of intense emotions and actions. I think another symbol for Scorpio is the mermaid, with her beautiful head and torso above the surface and her powerful tail beneath the surface. Siren, as she was often called, had a beautiful voice that made sailors abandon reason and steer their ships to the rocks. Victorian writers and artists were fascinated and repelled by the mermaid, to see a beautiful woman from the waist up and then to see her legs and her sexuality fused together in a powerful tail; did that mean she controlled her sexual activity? The power frightened them and the idea that they had no access to her sexuality bewildered them. They wrote about her and they painted her, but they never learned her secrets. Hans Christian Andersen tried to tame her by taking away her voice or her soul. A modern cartoon turns her into a calypso-singing redhead, a kind of fishy, singing doll baby. Nevertheless, the attraction of her mystery remains beneath the surface of the cartoon.

No matter how hard anyone tries, the mermaid remains a powerful symbol of watery mystery, the key to emotions, love, and sexual pleasure. She chooses when she sings, where she swims, and who sees her. Her mystery is revealed to only a few and her song often draws the unthinking into the shallows and the rocks.

Scorpios are mysterious and complex people, concerned with what is below the surface, the occult and intuitive worlds. Scorpios are intense and magnetic. Turned inward, Scorpios are destructive, obsessive, repressed, and cruel. Like the mermaid's song, Scorpio wit compels you and flails you. They are as harsh on themselves as they are on others. This intensity can bring deep transformations of the soul.

The Water Crone is intense as she taps into the deep mysteries of life. She is guided by her intuitive sense of what is right and what is wrong. She knows something and feels something rather than analyzing data. She knows life because she has lived long and felt much. She has felt intense rage at injustice and suffering. She has sought revenge. She has found life profoundly satisfying as she has loved with every fiber of her being. She has found life profoundly disappointing, as those she loves do not live up to her standards. She has fought for every iota of strength and wisdom in her life. Nothing has come easy for her. She has learned great peace and compassion. She knows of profound sorrow and intense happiness. She has earned her wisdom and has taken possession of her power. She is a great and knowing teacher, but she is not an easy one. With this sense of knowing she moves into action and into change. The deep waters of the ocean churn around her as she swims into our lives and transforms them. You can taste the salty tang of the ocean on the cuts she inflicts as she forces you to swim deeper into knowing. She sees beneath the surface and knows all the secrets. She expects the same of you and the same for you.

The Crone creates a tidal wave, moving swiftly into your life and changing everything. Tidal waves, like the other great acts of nature, profoundly change things. The ocean floor is churned up and sea flora is moved to other places. New fish and animals repopulate the water. Tidal waves crash onto land and destroy homes and businesses, but they also move the land and enrich the soil. Tidal waves revitalize an area and prevent the soil from being depleted.

The intense power of nature frightens us. If we look beyond that fright we know in an intuitive way that things like this happen for good reasons. In our brightly sunlit lives guided by the scientific method, we have been taught to know the facts and to understand what we learn from five of our senses. If we can see it, touch it, hear it, smell it, or taste it, then we can know it. If we cannot experience a truth with those senses, it is either suspect or it is wrong. There are other senses, including our intuition, that can help us see when there is no light, to hear when there is no sound, or to feel when there is no texture. We can touch with our minds and we can smell with our memories. We have been taught to disregard our intuitive sense and so we only have a portion of the tools available to us.

In the Dark Moon world, we can use our intuitive sense. More and more in this new age, we are learning to access and use our intuition. We learn to achieve a balance between the facts and what we know through our intuition. Victorian men could not find the answers of the mermaid because they could only touch, smell, hear, see, and taste. They did not extend their senses beyond their body so they could only paint her and write her. They never found what they sought because they did not have the language of intuition.

ℛ Swimming into the Deep
A Ritual for the Dark Moon in Scorpio

Creating Sacred Space: Spend some time using your intuitive awareness. When you meditate, dream, or daydream, do you see hear, smell, touch, or smell? More than one? Learn to distinguish between wishful thinking and intuitive awareness.

Casting the Circle: Sit in the middle of your circle and cast your awareness beyond where you are sitting. See with your third eye, the intuitive ocular sense. Hear your circle resonate with a single tone. Hum that tone until you feel your circle cast around you. "Blessed be."

Summoning the Guardians and the Elementals:

Summon the West:

Guardians of the Western Shore, watery spirits of the deep ocean, join me in my sacred circle. Undines,

playful swimmers of the deep, join me in my sacred
circle. Hail and welcome.

Summon the North:

Guardians of the Northern Shore, arctic spirits of
icy waters, join me in my sacred circle. Gnomes,
burrowers of the cold ground, join me in my sacred
circle. Hail and welcome.

Summon the East:

Guardians of the Eastern Shore, airy creatures of
windswept skies, join me in my sacred circle. Winged
Sylphs, fliers of the eastern sky, join me in my sacred
circle. Hail and welcome.

Summon the South:

Guardians of the Southern Shore, flaming spirits
of the tropical waters, join me in my sacred circle.
Salamanders, burning creatures of the flame. Join
me in my sacred circle. Hail and welcome.

Evoke the Goddess:

Yemaya, Ocean Goddess of deep purpose, bring
intuition and joy to my sacred circle. Hail and
welcome.

Evoke the God:

Neptune, god of the Ocean and all creatures that
swim, bring power and authority to my sacred circle.
Hail and welcome.

Center and Ground: You are standing at the edge of a river on
a shore filled with rocks that have been washed with water. The
rocks are smooth with decades of gentle washing. The water
washes over you, gently cleansing you of all that bothers you.
You become a rock, lying on that gentle shore as the waves wash

over you. Your feet, shins, and knees are rock. Your thighs, hips, and torso are rock. Your arms, hands, and head are rock. Feel your rockness lie among the rocks as the water washes over you. Feel the warmth of the earth beneath you as the earth connects with you. Feel the earth power down to the solid middle earth. Feel the sun reach down and caress your rockness and feel the energy through this sunbeam. Lie there connected to the earth and the sky above as the water washes over you. Open your eyes, connected to All That Is.

Statement of Ritual Intent:

Life often has an incomprehensibility about it that cannot be explained by our analytical sense that uses only the five senses of taste, smell, seeing, hearing, and touch. I am going to dive into the caves of the Water Crone to learn the deep wisdom of using my intuitive senses.

ଓ Meditation

Take three centering breaths, with the last one coming out in the same sound that cast your circle. Close your eyes. You are standing beneath the Dark Moon in a seaside grotto. You are standing high on a large rock above the ocean. You can hear the waves lapping against the rock-lined shore. You can taste the sharp tang of salt in the water sprayed from the waves and you can smell the stagnant smell of seaweed and saltwater. The stars above are reflected on the water's surface. You stretch your arms to the sky and thank Neptune for his presence and the guarantee of a safe journey. You dive headfirst into the water. You feel the exhilaration of almost-too-cold water against your skin. You taste the salt and feel the sting as the water connects with a cut or two. The water is welcoming you and calls you to swim deeper. You feel your two legs come together in a mermaid's tail. With a joyful splash of your powerful tail, you swim through the water. This is fun. Beautiful sea creatures surround you and guide you deeper. They whisper words of encouragement and love. They call you to swim deeper. You swim to the deepest cave at the center of the world, the Cave of the Water Crone. You enter the Cave. Out of the water emerges the Water Crone, who seats herself beside the water on a rocky ledge. "Hoist yourself up and sit by me," she says. You feel the intensity of her gaze as you do as she says. You are wonderfully graceful and powerful as you surge out of the waster and seat yourself on the ledge. The Water Crone looks deep into your eyes. She opens your intuition so that you may sense the Great Mystery.

She tells you a story.

When it is time, thank her for her wisdom. Give her a word, song, or story as a gift, for she treasures these things. Kiss her on the cheek and say goodbye. A great wave sweeps you off the ledge and carries you upward and forward. You are standing on your own two legs by the ocean pool. A light rain falls. Breathe three times. On the third breath, open your eyes.

Raising the Cone of Power: Remember the sound and rhythm of the waves of the ocean. Like the waves of the ocean, move and sing around your circle until you feel the power move through you and WHOOSH out into the Universe.

Cakes and Ale:
Great creatures of the Water, fresh and salt, thank you for the wisdom of knowing. As I eat and drink, I ground this wisdom into my being. Blessed be.

Dismiss the Guardians and the Elementals:

Dismiss the South:

> Flaming salamanders, thank you for the fire of will and sexuality. Go from my sacred circle with my thanks and my blessings. Guardians of the Southern Shore, thank you for the Will and the Mystery. Go from my sacred circle with my thanks and my blessings. Farewell.

Dismiss the East:

> Airy sylphs of the zephyrs, thank you for your vision and your dreams. Go from my sacred circle with my thanks and my blessings. Guardians of the Eastern Shore, thank you for the Knowing of the Mystery. Go from my sacred circle with my thanks and my blessings. Farewell.

Dismiss the North:

> Earthy Gnomes, thank you for the Body of Mystery. Go from my sacred circle with my thanks and my blessings. Guardians of the Northern Shore, thank you for the wisdom of Silent Mystery. Go from my sacred circle with my thanks and my blessings. Farewell.

Dismiss the West:

> Watery Undines, thank you for the love and the tests. Go from my sacred circle with my thanks and my blessings. Guardians of the Western Shore, thank your for the Daring Mystery. Go from my sacred circle with my thanks and my blessings. Farewell.

Dismiss the God:

> Mighty Neptune, God of the Trident, thank you for the power of the deep ocean. Go from my sacred circle with my thanks and my blessings. Farewell.

Dismiss the Goddess:

> Yemaya, Goddess of the water. Thank you for the
> Dark Knowing of Intuition. Thank you for the Joy
> of the Water and the Mystery of the Mermaid, which
> is my mystery. Go from my sacred circle with my
> thanks and my blessing. Farewell.

Center and Ground: Take three breaths and feel yourself as the rock, washed by the gentle lapping of the waves on the shore. Feel your connections to Middle Earth and feel the sun join you to the Universe above. Feel your connection to All That Is. Gently pull back from the earth until you are a rock again. Keep what energy you need and pull gently back from your connection with the sun. Let the water move over you one more time and know that you are always part of the One. Breathe three times and on the third breathe let out the tone of your circle and open your eyes.

Open the Circle: Sitting in the center of your circle, connect with the tone that surrounds you as your sacred circle. Hum it loudly and then hum it softly. Take the volume down, down, down until there is silence. "The circle is open but unbroken."

CR

Dark Moon in Sagittarius

The Dark Moon Path continues its unraveling as it bursts into the creative fire of Sagittarius. Fire was a spark in Aries, burst into flame in Leo, and moves into wildfire for Sagittarius. The Crone acts on the will and creativity in Sagittarius.

The Muses were the nine daughters of Zeus and the goddesses of Memory. Their nurse Eupheme and her son Crotus raised them on a mountain. Crotus sang, danced, and hunted with the nine Sisters, who represented the arts and heroic poetry. When Crotus died, the Muses asked Zeus to place him in the stars as a gesture of their love and gratitude. Zeus placed Crotus in the constellation of Sagittarius the Archer. The word "Sagittarius" is rooted in the Latin for arrow, a symbol of far-reaching vision, flying swiftly to the heart of the matter. The Archer is pictured as a centaur, a creature that is half-horse and half-human. The head, shoulders, and torso are human, encompassing the heart and brain of the creature, while the lower body and legs are that of a horse. The body power and sexuality is that of an animal. In myth, centaurs were the great teachers of the Greek youth. They were also powerful, graceful, and fast. When drunk, centaurs have an unsurpassed reputation for rowdiness and raunchiness, with great animal appetites for food, drink, and sex. While visionaries and intellectuals, centaurs were undeniably physical. One of the most famed centaurs, Chiron, was the teacher of the great including Hercules. Chiron is in the pantheon of Greek gods.

Sagittarius is an explorer, seeking the wonders of a mystical life. Like the arrow, Sagittarius seeks the spiritual heart of the matter, often wounding self and others in the process. A wounded healer is a profoundly powerful healer. In the process of the spiritual journey, a Sagittarius will be thoughtless, funny, charismatic, frustrating, benevolent, and irresponsible. The positive qualities of Sagittarius are hopeful, optimistic, jovial, expansive, sage-like, metaphysical, adventurous, frank, and freedom loving. The negative qualities are that Sagittarians wound with jokes, and are pompous, indolent, scatter-brained, and restless.

The Fire Crone takes her life experience and bounds forward, seeking adventure with a passion that is enthusiastic and youthful. Enthusiasm helps the Fire Crone remain youthful, even adolescent, well beyond her chronological years. It might seem that this Crone is not really a crone at all. She does bring a totality of life experience with her. The Fire Crone knows that life is too short to sit still and wait. She must act, move, and dance toward the Great Mystery.

As Sagittarius, the Fire Crone is between two very intense signs of the Zodiac, the brooding Scorpio and the serious Capricorn. By contrast, the Fire Crone may seem like "Crone Lite," with little substance. To believe that would be a big mistake. The Fire Crone has passion and fire in her being, not unlike the fire used in glassblowing. In glassblowing, two gasses are mixed together. One gas is intense, thin, and blue. You can run your hand through the stream of fire and not get burned, if you are quick. When you add sulphur, the flame becomes fatter, and more yellow. This flame will burn you. Together, the cold flame and the hot flame heat the glass until it is partially liquified. Then the glass can be manipulated or blown to shape great works of art or to shape utility items such as beakers and jars. A drop of dye will add color.

The Fire Crone will burn you with a flame that is hot or a flame that burns cold, in order to shape you into a work of art or to be what you need to be.

Wildfire is what characterizes the Fire Crone of Sagittarius. As with the other great acts of nature, the storm and the tidal waves, wildfire both destroys and creates. When a fire burns in a forest, it destroys the old growth. At the same time, new seeds are released to the ground that is no longer shaded from the sky. The sun reaches the seeds and they grow into new trees and other plants. This creates new habitat for creatures that live there or new species that move in. In addition to destroying, the wildfire creates new living spaces for the creatures of the earth.

With her fire, the Fire Crone brings us creativity. Many people, particularly women, tell me that they have no talent. Whatever is being discussed, I hear, "I wish I could do that but I have no talent." I have come to believe several things about that statement. One is that we have rigid ideas about what is art and what is creativity. With those expectations, we may not be able to duplicate the works of others. I also believe that we do not recognize talent and creativity. We need to learn to color outside the lines and expand our definition of creativity and talent.

Creativity is a magical approach to living. Magic is the creative part of Wicca. Because Wicca is a religion that celebrates life as sacred, creativity is based in celebration. All creativity is sacred because all creativity is life. I have a talent for organization. I can organize an event or service and make it happen, whether it is running a medium-sized college library or a large academic conference. I enjoy this activity very much. I spark to it and really get going. I can also tell you that no one is impressed or even thinks that organization is a talent. This particular talent is not drawing or singing with a beautiful voice, so it is often greeted with a ho-hum. I have learned not to care what other people think. It is something I enjoy, so onward I go like the arrow shooting forward.

Creativity is rooted in joy and open to the expectation that something will happen. It is optimistic and embracing. Creativity needs the optimism because creativity is risk and it takes courage to be different or to risk criticism. So dance, sing, organize, or do whatever gives you joy.

When the sun is about to leave Sagittarius, pagans celebrate the holiday of Yule, the winter solstice. This is the day when the night is the longest. The dark has overtaken the light and the sun shows its face only rarely. The world is stark and leafless, covered with snow. After solstice, the wheel of the year turns again and daylight begins to overtake the dark, and we know in our cells that spring is on its way. We go into the Dark for a winter's sleep, storing fat to nourish us and prepare for the rebirth of spring. We dream in the Dark of the Light that will come. We dream Hope.

♋ Arrow into the Heart
A Ritual for the Dark Moon in Sagittarius

Creating Sacred Space: Spend some time thinking about your creativity and life between the lines. How can you go outside the lines? Do you need to? What gives you the greatest joy?

Casting the Circle: Use something pretty like glitter or yarn or small scraps of colored paper and spread it in a circle around your sacred space, chanting three times, "A circle is cast."

Summoning the Guardians and the Elementals:

Summon the South:

> Fiery Guardians, Mothers and Fathers of the Southern Gate, bring will and desire to my sacred circle. Salamanders bring the imaginative fire of creativity to my sacred circle. Hail and welcome.

Summon the West:

> Watery Guardians, Grandmothers and Grandfathers of the Western gate, bring emotion and compassion to my sacred circle. Undines bring the cleansing power of water to my sacred circle. Hail and welcome.

Summon the North:

> Grounded Guardians, Crones and Sages of the Northern Gate, bring wisdom and stillness to my sacred circle. Gnomes, bring the fertile creativity of the earth to my sacred circle. Hail and welcome.

Summon the East:

> Airy Guardians, Sisters and Brothers of the Eastern Gate, bring youth and clarity to my sacred circle. Sylphs, bring the breezes of a sharp mind to my sacred circle. Hail and welcome.

Evoke the Goddess:

> Nine Muses, sisters on the mountaintop, bring the
> joy of creating beauty and fun to my sacred circle.
> Hail and welcome.

Evoke the God:

> Mighty Chiron, visionary and sensualist, bring the
> sense of pleasure and the vision of joy to my sacred
> circle. Hail and welcome.

Center and Ground: Breathe and stretch. Close your eyes. See yourself as a fallen tree at the edge of a sunlit meadow. Feel your body connect with the earth. Feel your toes connect with the earth, feel your legs connect with the earth, feel your hips connect with the earth, feel your torso connect with the earth, feel your neck and head connect with the earth, feel your arms connect with the earth. Feel the sun reach down and warm you. Feel the connection with the sky and with the Universe above. You are connected to the earth and to the Universe. Blessed be.

Statement of Ritual Intent:

> Creativity is rooted in joy. Joy is the assurance that
> no matter what the surface events, happy or sad, I am
> happy, assured that the Universe is not only a safe
> place, but also a place where we belong. Joy grows
> within me and roots around my heart so that I am
> free to express myself in whatever way gives me joy.
> Life is magic! I am magic!

○ℛ Meditation

*You are standing at the edge of the forest and you can feel
that it is a very old forest. You can feel the calm wisdom
of the old trees growing in harmony with the earth and
creatures around them. You notice a path before you and
you walk through the forest. You come to the edge of the*

forest. Before you there is a landscape devastated by forest fire. You see new plants growing on the ground and realize this new life is in contrast to the burnt trees reaching toward the sun. Under one of these burnt trees, you see a centaur. You walk to the centaur, who turns to greet you. In the greeting, the centaur gives you the gift of its name. Keep it as a talisman of magic for you. Talk to the centaur. The centaur will share joyous wonders with you. Then the centaur will draw its bow and arrow and say to you, "Climb onto my arrow." You climb onto the arrow and find that you fit perfectly. The centaur draws back the bow and feels the arrow straighten toward its mark. You feel a fearsome excitement well up inside you and as it seems to burst from you, the arrow bursts from the bow, flying smoothly high and long through the air. Notice what is around you. You land and discover you are at the heart of your joy. Look around and drink in the sights. Near your left hand, you see a gift that symbolizes your creativity. Pick it up and keep it to remind you that creativity is joy and it is yours. Breathe three times and on the third breath, open your eyes.

Raising the Cone of Power: In your pretty glittery circle, say the name of your centaur over and over again. Get louder and faster as you move to the rhythm of that name. Keep moving, faster and louder, until you feel the power move through you and WHOOSH out into the Universe.

Cakes and Ale:

Great and creative powers, thank you for the wonderful joy of creativity. Thank you for the vision of wonder and magic. Blessed be.

Center and Ground: Return to the sunny meadow. Disconnect yourself gently from the ground. Feel the sun reaching down to you. Gently disconnect yourself, saving the energy that you need. Blessed be.

Dismiss the God:

> Magical Chiron, strong centaur, God of Vision,
> thank you for the joy you brought to my sacred circle.
> Farewell.

Dismiss the Goddess:

> Merry Muses, the Nine Goddesses of Art and Poetry,
> thank you for the vision of talent and beauty. Thank
> you for the joy you bring to my sacred circle.
> Farewell.

Dismiss the Guardians and Elementals:

Dismiss the East:

> Sylphs, keepers of the passionate mind, thank you for
> the clear you bring to my sacred circle. Guardians of
> the Airy Eastern Gate, thank you for the brilliance of
> creativity. All go from my sacred circle with my
> thanks and my blessings.

Dismiss the North:

> Gnomes of the ground and stone, thank you for the
> dark wisdom of the ground. Earthy Guardians of the
> Northern Gate, thank you for the quiet joy you bring
> to my sacred circle. All go from my sacred circle with
> my thanks and my blessings. Farewell.

Dismiss the West:

> Undines, diving deep into the heart, thank you for
> the compassion you bring to my sacred circle.
> Guardians of the Western Gate, thank you for the

emotions you bring to my sacred circle. All go from
my sacred circle with my blessings and my thanks."

Dismiss the South:

Salamanders, bright flaming passions, thank you for
the desire to create. Fiery Guardians of the Southern
Gate, thank you for the brilliant fire of art that you
bring to my sacred circle. All go from my sacred
circle with my thanks and my blessings. Farewell.

Open the Circle: Going widdershins, sweep away the circle
with your outstretched arms. Chant, "The circle is open but
unbroken" three times.

CR

Dark Moon in Capricorn

The Dark Moon Path unravels its dark spiral in Capricorn, the Earth Crone. Earth was soil in Taurus, a mountain in Virgo, and moves swiftly into action as earthquake in Capricorn. The Crone acts with power in Capricorn.

The sign of Capricorn is one of the most intense of the Zodiac. The story of the goat sign, Capricorn begins before the gods of Olympus, during the time of the Titans. Kronos, the king of the Titans, was terrified that one of his children would challenge his position as king of the gods and overthrow him. Rhea, known as "She of the Sacred Oak," his wife (who was also his sister), bore Kronos a son. Knowing of Kronos' intense fear, she swaddled a stone and presented it to him as his new son.

Kronos swallowed the stone, thinking that he had gotten rid of his dangerous son. Rhea hid Zeus away in the mountains of Crete where he was raised by the goat Amaltheia and her sisters. She fed him milk and honey and Zeus grew strong and powerful. When he became an adult, he returned home and killed his father and began calling himself the Father of the Gods. When Amaltheia died, he placed her among the stars, which became the constellation Capricorn. He also used one of her horns as the cornucopia, the horn of plenty, which was always filled with whatever food and drink its holder desired. The cornucopia remains a symbol of unending abundance.

Further back in time, Zeus was a minor Cretan deity and Amaltheia and her sisters were actually healer priestesses serving the goddess Rhea. The Sacred Oak was revered, in part, because it supported the mistletoe, which was used extensively in healing and in sacred ritual. The story of Capricorn celebrates the abundance of the earth and the healing power of the natural world.

Capricorns are exceptionally grounded and are often called "stick-in-the-muds" when they get stubborn. They are practical, cautious, and realistic, not given to flights of fancy. They are demanding, wanting perfection before action is taken.

The Earth Crone is the Crone of Harvest. She knows of the abundance of the earth and the healing power of the world as well as she knows that the earth dies in the winter. She knows that the dead enrich the soil and set the groundwork for the birth of spring. The Crone sees the big picture of life and death and rebirth. She sees the Dark at the darkest time of year and knows that growth will happen, though not now.

Like the other Crones, the Earth Crone is a woman of action. The Crone grows in power and strength throughout her life and one day she accepts the power and decides to use it. She uses "I" as a strong, authentic use of personal power, dearly bought.

Bringing together experience and acceptance is an act of incredible power. The Earth Crone is a strong, inexorable force and it is her choice how she uses that power.

We have seen the incredible power of the natural world in storms, tidal waves, wildfires, and earthquakes. Each of these has two sides, destruction and construction. We have seen or experienced the power of earthquakes. The earth moves with incredible force, and buildings, bridges, and dams are destroyed. Earthquakes also create new landscapes. Volcanic earthquakes form islands—these become populated with new animals, including humans.

The Earth Crone has that incredible power. How she uses power is her choice. The Earth Crone may come into our life and totally disrupt it with a word or observation. She may provide us with a smooth ground to walk upon. She creates new landscapes in our hearts and our souls so that we may claim our own power.

Analysis and conversations about power and its uses have been central to feminist concerns since the beginning of the modern feminist movement. Women began thinking about power and exposing its uses and abuses by patriarchal society. Books and tapes appeared to help women and others explore power and its nature. Readers were told how to use power to their advantage, how to recover from being overpowered, and how to combat the abuses of power. In her books *Dreaming the Dark* and *Truth or Dare* (Boston: Beacon Press, 1984; New York: Harper & Row, 1987), Starhawk began to talk about power from a spiritual perspective. Those books helped me answer the question, "How does a spiritual person use power for the good of all and the harm of none?" Starhawk says there are three types of power: *power-over* which has one person having power over another person, persons, or beings; *power-with* which is a partnering of people to use power, ideally in a more humane and democratic way; and *empowerment*, which I also call *power-with-*

in, which is a sense of authority that comes from inside and is born of a sense of worth.

We have all experienced power-over in school, at work, and in our families. Often we are placed in a situation where we must use power-over and it can be done without abusing others. However, it is very easy to move into abuse, whether it is just thoughtlessly making a decision without thinking of others or by consciously exerting power to control or hurt others. In power-over there is the powerful one and there are others. It is YOU and I, but never WE.

Power-with is based in the thinking that everyone involved is part of the decision making. It is based in WE. We are in this together. It is a partnership that needs constant check-ups and constant conversations. Whether it is a family or a business, it is a good way to operate because everyone feels a part of the situation and a part of the outcome. I am involved in participatory management and one of the ways I characterize it is that it is all talk, talk, talk, and more talk. Power-with takes time.

Empowerment is a sense of personal power that stems from a personal sense of worth. To be able to say with authority and strength "I" is a powerful statement of worth. Webweaver has said there is another power called power-in-spite-of. I think that is another part of empowerment where someone's sense of personal power is so strong and so positive that they can succeed despite all the garbage that life throws at them. The ability to take your power to say "I" and then add a verb is a powerful action. The Crone makes these statements with the authority of her truth.

ᑳ I
Ritual for the Dark Moon in Capricorn

Creating Sacred Space: Spend some time thinking about power in your life. Can you identify power as it plays out as power-over, power-with, and empowerment? What is your role? How would you like power to play out in your life?

Casting the Circle: If you can and you do not mind the clean up, take some soil and spread it around your circle (if not, carry it in a clear bowl). Move three times clockwise, chanting, "A circle is cast."

Summoning the Guardians and the Elementals:

Summon the North:

> Sages and Crones of the North, silent and wise, listeners when the soul speaks, join me in my sacred circle. Gnomes, burrowers to the Center of Life, join me in my sacred circle. Hail and welcome.

Summon the East:

> Maidens and Youths of the East, moving and knowing, seers of the clear vision of the mind, join me in my sacred circle. Sylphs, flyers into the winds of change, join me in my sacred circle. Hail and welcome.

Summon the South:

> Amazons and Warriors of the South, passionate fighters for what the will desires, join me in my sacred circle. Salamanders, burning and creating, join me in my sacred circle. Hail and welcome.

Summon the West:

> Mothers and Fathers of the West, loving and forgiving, feeling the truth when the heart cries.

Join me in my sacred circle. Undines, divers into the heart of emotion, join me in my sacred circle. Hail and welcome.

Evoke the Goddess:

Cerridwen, Moon lady of the Cauldron of Life and Death, Sage Guardian of the Life and Death, bring your wisdom and your power. Join me in my sacred circle.

Evoke the God:

Herne the Hunter, horned one, Lord of the Wild and the Wild Hunt, bring your courage and your daring and join me in my sacred circle. Hail and welcome.

Center and Ground: You are standing in the middle of a great rocky mountain range. Before you is a ledge of stone that reaches deep into the earth. Lie down upon the ledge and feel your consciousness merge with the rock. Feel your body melt into the rock and become rock. Feel the connectedness to the rock as it goes down to the center of the Earth. Feel the mountain above you reach for the sky and feel yourself merge with that mountain. Feel the energy in your body as it goes through the mountain into your body and to the rock below the surface. Know that you are connected and linked to the earth and to the sky.

Statement of Ritual Intent:

The acceptance of personal power is a transforming experience of combining acceptance with knowledge and experience. I am all that I have experienced and I am all that I know. I am a person who has value and the right to act and to speak. This transforms me in ways that are exciting and even unimaginable.

℞ Meditation

You are standing on a plain beneath the Full Moon.
Before your eyes, the moon cycles through from full to
waning and dark. You see the goat outlined in stars above
you as your vision acclimates to the Dark. Suddenly the
earth begins to shake. You are in the middle of an earth-
quake. You are tossed around a little bit. Experience the
magnificent power of the Earth and do not be afraid.
Suddenly you are tossed upward into the dark night sky
until you are in the midst of the stars. You fall gently
downward to the top of a mountain. Before you is the
Healer Priestess Amaltheia. Her cloak is made of
goatskins and she carries an oak staff around which is a
vine of mistletoe with its white berries and green leaves.
She embraces you and calls you "Sister." She talks with
you and tells you the truth in your heart. You feel her
gathering her power about her and she stands tall and
you stand tall before her.

She reaches into your body with her hands and pulls
something out. What did that feel like? She holds out her
hands filled with what she pulled from your body. "This
is your power," she says to you, "Listen while I tell you
about your power." Gaze at your power and listen to her
wisdom.

When she is done, she puts your power back in your
hands. Around you she puts a goatskin coat, the sign that
you are indeed her sister. She brings out the cornucopia.
From it you pull the gift you need most, that which will
help you claim your power.

It is time to go. Reach in the pocket of your new cloak
and pull out a gift for her. Give it to her with your thanks

and your blessings. Say goodbye. Gaze up at the moon
and breathe once. Breathe again. On the third breath,
open your eyes.

Raising the Cone of Power: Take some time to absorb what you have been given and the STAND UP and march around your sacred circle. Merge the march as a dance. Start chanting softly and then get louder. Chant, "I, I, I, I, I, I, I, I, I, I, I," until you feel the power rush up through you and WHOOSH into the Universe.

Cakes and Ale:

Amaltheia, Healer Priestess and wise guide to
my power, thank you for your wisdom and the
knowledge that I have gained today. I say this prayer
in thanksgiving for the gifts I have been given today.
Blessed be.

Eat and drink so that you can ground this experience into your body and your everyday reality.

Dismiss the Guardians and the Elementals:

Dismiss the West:

Undines, magic dolphins, and eels, thank you for
the wisdom to know the heart of power. Fathers and
Mothers of the West, thank you for your love and
nurturing. All go from my sacred circle with my
thanks and my blessings. Farewell.

Dismiss the South:

Salamanders, firebirds, and dragons, thank you for
the wisdom to know the passion of power. Warriors
and Amazons of the South, thank you for your
energy and will. All go from my sacred circle with
my thanks and my blessings. Farewell.

Dismiss the East:

> Sylphs, flying ones, thank you for the wisdom to
> know the mind of power. Youths and maidens of the
> East, thank you for your knowing. All go from my
> sacred circle with my thanks and my blessings.
> Farewell.

Dismiss the North:

> Gnomes, thank you for the wisdom to understand the
> body of power. Sages and Crones of the North, wise
> and powerful, thank you for your silence. All go from
> my sacred circle with my thanks and my blessings.
> Farewell.

Open the Circle: Going widdershins or counterclockwise
around the circle, make sweeping motions with your hands as
you open the circle. Chant, "The circle is open but unbroken"
three times.

∞

The Action of the Dark Crone

The Crone is not at war with life or with anyone in it. Neither does she surrender to the process of aging or to anything else. The Crone knows much. She knows that life is short and life is too long. She knows that good things happen and bad things happen. She knows that every fault is evidence of a hidden strength and that every strength has a flaw. She understands that life has a complexity to it that defies explanation so we take refuge in dualities. She knows that life has a simplicity and synchronicity to it that is comforting and disrupting.

The Crone knows, to her comfort and to her dismay, that to build things, we must often destroy things. With construction comes destruction. I'm fond of saying, "I don't need a house to fall on me, but what is all this rubble around here?!!" When the wall falls or is pushed over by the Crone, she knows it can and will be rebuilt.

It will not be rebuilt in the way that it was before and that is the purpose of the Crone. She is a transformative agent that destroys and constructs in the same action. That dual action creates something new and newly imagined. This action and purpose is not done out of anger, it is done with love. It is done with a love so large that it encompasses all that is. It embraces us and transforms us and brings us into the love of the Divine.

The Crone stirs the Cauldron of Life and Death and transforms it all.

The Dark Weaver

The Dark Weaver

The Weaver takes the lessons of the Maiden, Mother, and Crone and puts them together in a pattern. Even though the Crone has the long view of life, love, and death, the Weaver goes beyond transformation into creating patterns of magic and mystery. She takes the synergy of the Maiden, the mystery of the Mother, and the action of the Crone and weaves it all together into a pattern that is unseen by the Maiden, Mother, and Crone because they are either in the midst of it or too close to it. The Weaver weaves the Dark, weaves the Light, weaves death and life together to create, transform, and make new patterns and paths.

The Weaver goes beyond ego and desire into connection. The Weaver moves all the so-called bad qualities and the so-called good qualities into a pattern that flows with the Universe and with the Divine that is ultimately Love. The Weaver encompasses it all, and while we may be able to see individual threads, we must stand back to see the whole. It is beautiful, wild, and beyond belief. The greatest thing of all that it is—it is you.

Dark Moon in Arachne

The Dark Moon Path goes into the darkest of the Dark, Arachne. Arachne is unexplored territory and we are pioneers. The thirteenth sign of the Zodiac was so fearsome that it was written out of the one that is in common usage in the modern world.

Where did the idea of Arachne come from? It is not in the Zodiac that we know in the twentieth and twenty-first centuries. There are thirteen moons in a calendar year, yet there are just twelve signs of the Zodiac. In 1977, John Vogh wrote *Arachne Rising: The Search for the Thirteenth Sign of the Zodiac* (New York, Doubleday, 1977). In this book, he gives a short history of the development of Zodiacs, for there are more than the one we know now. The one we use today was adopted in the

135

Greek and Roman times and has remained relatively unchanged since those times. This Zodiac is a solar Zodiac, based on the movement of the sun through the skies during one set of seasons, one year.

Other cultures had other Zodiacs and other symbols, including Zodiacs based on lunar time, the movement of the moon through the seasons. Those Zodiacs had thirteen symbols. The Greeks and the Romans who founded their philosophy on logic and reason considered thirteen an unreasonable number. Thirteen is more appropriate to the realm of dreams and the subconscious and is inappropriate to the sunlit world of logic, technological advancement, and science.

Vogel proposed that the thirteenth sign was that of psychic ability and that the symbol be that of Arachne, the Spider. I have adapted that for the Dark Moon Path to name the thirteenth moon. When *Sisters of the Dark Moon* was a correspondence course, Arachne appeared near the end of the journey for two years, and in the middle for one year. Arachne will move according to the pattern of the Moon as she dances through the sky and through our lives. Just as our lives change in a moment because of a death, a birth, an accident, a bequest, or a joke, Arachne is not stationary. She moves according to the great pattern of the Universe.

The story of Arachne is from the Greek. Arachne was a human woman of superlative talent. She was a spinner and a weaver—her tapestries were of unsurpassed beauty and intricacy, considered the most beautiful in the world. She entered a contest to create the most beautiful tapestry and she won. Her competition was Athena, Goddess of Wisdom and of War. Athena, beaten by a human woman, was offended by Arachne's lack of humility in the presence of the Divine, and so turned Arachne into a spider. The spider has woven beautiful, unique, and fragile designs ever since.

Many, many cultures use the spider as a symbol for Fate or the Goddess. Some Native American cultures have Spider Grandmother who weaves the pattern of life and death. The web of the spider has symbolized fragility and beauty, and a trap as we step into the parlor of the spider. We also learn from *Charlotte's Web* (E. B. White, HarperCollins, 1997), where Charlotte the spider is a wonderful, loving, and encouraging friend and teacher. Through her death and the life of her spider children we see the continuity of life and, most especially, love.

The one thing we can learn from Arachne, the Weaver, is love. The pattern is woven with love and includes love, all kinds of love, and *is* love.

It is love that transforms us. Other emotions change us. Anger certainly changes us. Sorrow and grief change us. Loving transformation encompasses all our lessons, all our mistakes, and all our triumphs into one Divine pattern. We are that Divine. When pagans and Wiccans say, "You are Goddess, You are God," they mean (or at least I mean) that we are that pattern of the Divine. It is not wishful thinking, it is what we are.

We accomplish the weaving of the pattern in the Spirit. In past chapters, we have looked at the separate elements of earth, air, water, and fire. In Arachne we are in the element of the Spirit which is all of those elements and beyond. Since we are spiritual beings, we know what that is, even though we may not be able to articulate it clearly. In the element of the Spirit, we learn that "as above, so below" means that we are not just reflections of the Divine, but we are Divine, and the Divine is as much a reflection of us as we are of the Divine. It is a Great Mystery.

❧ Weaving the Dark
A Ritual for the Dark Moon in Arachne

Creating Sacred Space: Spend time thinking about what you have learned about the Dark. Do not dwell on what you have and have not done. What remains part of the unexplored for you? What have you embraced that was not there before? What are the patterns that are Divine?

Cast the Circle: Use your body to cast the circle. Imagine a strong, thick, dark line around your sacred space as you walk clockwise three times around the circle.

Summon the Guardians and the Elementals:

Summon the East:

> Guardians of the darkest dawn, bring knowing to my sacred circle. Sylphs of the dark morning, bring clarity to my sacred circle. Hail and welcome.

Summon the South:

> Guardians of the fierce noon, bring will to my sacred circle. Salamanders of the relentless day, bring passion to my sacred circle. Hail and welcome.

Summon the West:

> Guardians of the dark sunset, bring love to my sacred circle. Undines of the dark sunset sea, bring love to my sacred circle. Hail and welcome.

Summon the North:

> Guardians of the darkest midnight, of the witching hour, bring wisdom to my sacred circle. Gnomes of the dark earth, bring silence to my sacred circle. Hail and welcome.

Evoke the Goddess:

> Spider Goddess, Arachne, Grandmother, Weaver of
> our Fates and our Divine Love, join me in my sacred
> circle, with love. Hail and welcome.

Evoke the God:

> Great Hades, Lord of the Dark and of the Forge that
> makes us Divine, join me in my sacred circle. Hail
> and welcome.

Center and Ground: Take three deep, cleansing breaths. With
the last, close your eyes and sit or lie down. Scan your body. As
you look at your toes you see that you are rock. As you look at
your knees, thighs, pelvis, you are rock. As you look at your
torso, shoulders, and arms, you are rock. As you look at your
head, you are rock. Stay in your rock being and know the calm
slow life of a rock as it sits on Mother Earth. Feel the warmth of
the earth seep up through your being. Feel the warmth of the sun
as the air surrounds you, connecting you with the Universe. Sit
for a minute in the warmth of the earth and the sun, and know
you are connected to All That Is.

Statement of Ritual Intent:

> My intent is to think over my time as a Sister on the
> Dark Moon Path, to feel all that I have learned and
> to cherish all that I have become. I intend to
> embrace the Dark.

○੭ Meditation

*You are settled and centered in yourself. You are standing
in the middle of a great plain under a Full Moon. As you
gaze at the sky, you see that the moon cycles through all
the phases. Now you are standing at the Dark Moon, the
moon at her Darkest. Your senses are alert. You hear*

*voices calling out to you. They tell you what you have
learned. You hear other voices. They tell you what is still
in the Dark, uncherished and uncared for. Soon one voice
distinguishes itself from the others, and you see standing
before you the Weaver, She who weaves You. The other
voices silence as she embraces you and welcomes you to
this great place. She speaks to you and tells you about the
pattern that you are weaving.*

*She tells you of love as well. When it is time, she will
embrace you again and send you on your way. Before
you go, tell her you love her, that you love. That is the
greatest gift and the greatest pattern.*

*She moves back into the Dark, always there for you.
Take three breaths and open your eyes, back in yourself.*

Raise the Cone of Power: Find a word or symbol to express
what you have learned to weave into your being. Imagine that
word or symbol engraved upon your hands. Weave your hands
back and forth in front of you in a pattern. Extend that movement to your arms, then your torso and head, then your whole
body. You are dancing the pattern around the circle. Faster and
faster until you feel the pattern move up thorough your body and
WHOOSH into the Universe.

Cakes and Ale:

Thank you for the pattern of love and life. Thank
you for the Dark, thank you for Me and I am the
Dark. Blessed be.

Center and Ground: See yourself as that rock sitting there on
the Earth. Feel the power of above and below go through you.
Ever so gently and keeping what you need, disconnect yourself
from the power of the sun. Ever so gently and keeping what you

need, disconnect yourself from the power of the Earth. Know
that you can have access to this power any time that you want.

Dismiss the God:

> Great Hades, the great god of the Dark, thank you
> for your wisdom in my sacred circle. Go with my
> thanks and my blessings. Hail and Farewell.

Dismiss the Goddess:

> Arachne, shining one, thank you for the patterns of
> love and life. Thank you for your presence in my
> sacred circle. Go with my thanks and my blessings.
> Hail and Farewell.

Dismiss the Directions:

Dismiss the North:

> Guardians and Gnomes of the North, thank you for
> your wisdom and silence. Thank you for the blessings
> on this path. Thank you and go with my blessings.
> Hail and Farewell.

Dismiss the West:

> Guardians and Undines of the West, thank you for
> your love and embrace. Thank you for the blessings
> on this path. Thank you and go with my blessings.
> Hail and Farewell.

Dismiss the South:

> Guardians and Salamanders of the South, thank you
> for your passion and your will. Thank you for the
> blessings on this path. Thank you and go with my
> blessings. Hail and Farewell.

Dismiss the East:

> Guardians and sylphs of the East, thank you for your
> clarity. Thank you for the blessings on this path.

Thank you and go with my blessings. Hail and
Farewell.

Open the Circle: Moving widdershins, open the circle by
moving three times around it. Blessed be.

CR

Patterns in the Dark

It has been quite a journey; thirteen moons and fourteen rituals. Different themes to explore, different aspects of the Goddess to know. The Dark is a special place that embraces us. It is like an attic. We store things there that we think we do not want or do not need. We store things that were given to us that we did not like or did not appreciate. Often, we neglect the attic, never visiting it and never cleaning it. Then one day, we climb the stairs with a small inadequate light to explore and look for things. We find a treasure trove of objects, small mysteries, and odd bits. We look and wonder, "Who is in that picture?" "Why did I put this here, I should put it in my bedroom." "I did not realize this would become so valuable." And so on.

Through the lunar year, we explore those things we have put in the attic. Our body, our intuition, and all the things we have studied help us see ourselves fully as human and as Divine. Our understanding grows as we look at each element as it grows from the smallest to the fullest power.

Fire is alive in us and in the Goddess as it grows from the first spark to bursting creativity in the wildfire. As the fire burns within us, we take on our full power as a being of infinite imagination and ability. Water flows as

143

a drop until it bursts from us as an inexorable wave of immense power. By tapping our intuition and by combining it with our emotions, we become mature beings, confident in our ability to handle life in all its bitterness and sweetness. Air blows gently into our lives and grows to become a hurricane of immense power. We step into that power and become agents of transformation and change. Earth welcomes our first tentative roots into her soil and we become a mountain of strength and power. We become the mountain and nothing can stand against us.

The Weaver takes the elements and braids them into us as a pattern of joy and hope. Taking the elements and the aspects of the Goddess and combining them with the lessons we have bravely faced in the Dark, we work with the Weaver as co-creators of our lives, reflecting the beauty of the Dark Moon.

The Goddess shows us her Dark face when the moon cycles to the darkest quarter, but she does not turn her face away. She shows us an intuitive world where we feel our way with our extrasensory senses, finding our way with trust and with love. It is a respite from the unrelenting light of the sunlight and the illumination of the Full Moon. We feel the patterns in our blood and in our bones rather than seeing them with our eyes. We touch the patterns with our living every day, and with the love we show others.

The Dark Moon Path weaves a wondrous path of the heart, of wisdom and joy of our physical, emotional, and spiritual life.

Blessed be and long may you weave the patterns of the Dark.

CR

Glossary

Amaltheia: In Greek myth, the goat who raised Zeus on Crete when he was hiding from the murderous intent of his father Kronos.

Aphrodite: The Greek Goddess of Love and Sexuality.

Aquarius: An air sign of the Zodiac, January 20–February 18, symbolized by the a man bearing a water vessel.

Arachne: In Greek myth, Arachne challenged Athena to a weaving contest and won. Athena punished her for arrogance by changing her into a spider. In this work, Arachne is the thirteenth sign of the Zodiac.

Aries: A fire sign of the Zodiac, March 21–April 19, symbolized by a ram.

Artemis: Greek Goddess of the Moon and the Night, of women in labor, and of the hunt and wild animals.

Beltane: Neo-pagan and Wiccan holiday celebrating love and sexuality on May 1.

Blessed be: Greeting and blessing used by Wiccans and neo-pagans.

Brigid: Celtic Goddess of the Forge.

Cancer: A water sign of the Zodiac, June 22–July 22, symbolized by a crab.

Capricorn: An earth sign of the Zodiac, December 22–January 19, symbolized by a goat.

Centaur: In Greek and Roman myth, a creature with the head and torso of a human and the lower body of a horse. Thought to be great teachers and great sensualists.

Center: A term used in ritual to calm the emotions and spirits, readying the person for the sacred work. This is accomplished by breathing and moving thought and attention to the center of a person's being.

Cerridwen: Celtic goddess of education, knowledge, and creativity. Considered a Destroyer of Life which was symbolized by her cauldron.

Chiron: The wise centaur who taught many of the Greek heroes, including Achilles and Hercules.

Circle: Ritual and worship in neo-pagan and Wiccan practice is done in a circle to symbolize the endless nature of the Divine. The term can also be used to refer to the group rather than using the term "coven."

Cone of Power: In ritual, the cone of power is raised by chant, movement, and song and moved into the universe. This is done to solidify and sanctify the work done and the ritual, and to make it a real change in the Universe.

Cornucopia: Also called "the horn of plenty" to symbolize abundance, the horn of Zeus' beloved goat nurse was used to symbolize the harvest.

Crone: One of the three aspects of the Goddess' life, the elder woman who has ceased to menstruate. Considered so powerful she can keep her blood inside.

Dark: That part of life which is without light. Often associated with the bad or evil side of life but is really a time of contemplation, meditation, and healing.

Demeter: Greek Goddess of Agriculture, mother to Persephone. When her daughter was kidnapped by Hades, God of the Underworld, Demeter went into a mourning so severe that it caused all life to be bleak (winter).

Deosil: Literally "sun-wise," and used to refer to the clockwise movement around the circle during ritual.

Descent: Part of the stories of many goddess who go down into the Underworld or land of the dead to retrieve a loved one.

Dionysus: Greek god of wine and of the vine. Also symbolized as the vegetative god who lives for a season and dies for a season.

East: One of the four directions summoned during ritual, also the element of air. East symbolizes the mind, learning, and thinking. The East is symbolized by the dawn, by spring, by flying animals and birds, and by light pastel colors such as pink and blue.

Elementals: Magical creatures found on this plane of existence and corresponding with the four directions and the four elements used in neo-pagan and Wiccan practice. Powerful, amoral, and playful, these creatures symbolize the raw power of that direction and element. See Sylphs, Gnomes, Undines, and Salamanders.

Equinox: The two days of the year, in the spring and in the fall, when the length of the day and the night are an equal number of minutes. In neo-pagan and Wiccan practice, these two are holidays, symbolizing balance.

Ereshkigal: Sumerian Goddess of the Night and of the Moon, Queen of the Underworld, Destroyer of Life.

Eros: Greek God of erotic love, symbolized by a little boy.

Evoke: In ritual, the term used for summoning the spirits, the Goddess, and the God to join the celebrants in the ritual.

Four Elements: In neo-pagan and Wiccan ritual the qualities that symbolize all of life: air, water, earth, and fire.

Four Directions: In neo-pagan and Wiccan ritual, East, West, North, and South are corners of the Universe summoned for the work. Also referred to as the Four Quarters.

Gaia: In Greek myth, the primordial Mother, the symbol of the earth and the world.

Ganymede: In Greek myth, the youth who served as the cup bearer to the gods, and Zeus' lover. After his death, became the constellation Aquarius.

Gemini: An air sign of the Zodiac, May 21–June 21, symbolized by human twin youths, usually male.

Gnomes: Elemental creatures of the earth. They do not look like the garden gnomes of popular culture.

Green Man: Celtic vegetative god of the hunt.

Ground: The neo-pagan and Wiccan practice of connecting with the earth. Serves to stabilize the celebrant when doing magical work.

Guardians: The powerful beings from otherworldly planes that willingly come when summoned to the ritual.

Hades: Greek God of the Dead, King of the Underworld.

Hecate: Greek Goddess of Moon and the Night, a Crone goddess who guards the crossroads.

Hera: Greek goddess of family, wife of Zeus, often very jealous and vengeful of his infidelities.

Herne: Celtic God of the Hunt and of wild animals.

Imbolc: The neo-pagan and Wiccan holiday celebrating Brigid and the early growth of the seeds, February 1.

Inanna: Sumerian goddess, Queen of the Heavens.

Invoke: In neo-pagan and Wiccan ritual practice, the God and/or Goddess is called to inhabit the body of the priest and priestess.

Iris: Greek goddess of the Rainbow, a messenger.

Kali Ma: Hindu goddess of Life and Death.

Kronos: King of the Titans, the gods who were the parents of the Greek gods, killed by his son Zeus.

Lammas: One of the holidays practiced by Wiccans and neo-pagans, celebrating the beginning of harvest.

Leo: A fire sign of the Zodiac, July 23–August 22, symbolized by a lion.

Libra: An air sign of the Zodiac, September 23–October 23, symbolized by scales.

Lunar year: Measuring time from moon to moon. There are thirteen moons in the solar calendar.

Maiden: One of the three aspects of the Goddess' life, this is the time of youth, often premenarche.

Midsummer: In neo-pagan and Wiccan practice, one of the Solstice holidays symbolizing the joyful youth of the God and Goddess.

Moon phases: The cycles of the moon from dark to full, occurring within a month.

Mother: One of the three aspects of the Goddess' life, this is the time after menarche and celebrates the ability to create life.

Muses: The nine Greek goddesses of creativity and art.

Mystery: In spiritual and religious practice, the term used to describe the Unknown and our spiritual understanding toward the Divine.

Neo-pagan: An umbrella term for the earth-based religions that have emerged in the twentieth century, including Druids, goddess worshipers, Wiccan, and others.

Neptune: Roman God of the Sea.

North: In neo-pagan and Wiccan practice, one of the directions summoned to represent the powers of the Universe. North is symbolized by earth and is represented by burrowing creatures, midnight, mountains, rocks, and soil.

Pagan: Often used interchangeably with neo-pagan, designation for practitioners of earth-based religions.

Pisces: A water sign of the Zodiac, February 19–March 20, symbolized by two fish swimming in a circle.

Poseidon: Greek God of the Sea.

Prometheus: In Greek myth, the God who gave fire (and enlightenment) to humans and is eternally punished by Zeus.

Ra: Egyptian God of the Sun.

Rhea: Queen of the Titans, wife of Kronos and mother of Zeus.

Ritual: The form of worship practiced by neo-pagans and Wiccans and is often free-formed and designed by the participants.

Sagittarius: A fire sign of the Zodiac, November 22–December 21, symbolized by a centaur with a bow and arrow.

Salamanders: The elemental associated with the South and with fire. Does not look like a lizard.

Samhain: The most important holiday in the neo-pagan and Wiccan calendar, celebrates the dead and connections with the ancestors as well as the end of harvest, October 31.

Scorpio: A water sign of the Zodiac, October 24–November 21, symbolized by a scorpion.

Sekhmet: Egyptian goddess of the sacred mysteries.

Shamanic: Refers to the modern practice of spiritual journey work facilitated by drumming or other steady beat. Derived from research into indigenous cultures in South America and elsewhere. The term "shaman" comes from Laplanders' spiritual leader and healer.

Solstice: One of two times a year. In the summer (Midsummer) it is the longest day of the year; in the winter (Yule) the shortest day of the year. Holidays for neo-pagans and Wiccans.

South: One of the four directions called into ritual by neo-pagans and Wiccans. South is symbolized by fire and noon. South is represented by the sun.

Spider: A powerful symbol of fate in several cultures. The ability to weave patterns makes the spider a creator.

Sylphs: One of the elemental creatures representing air.

Taurus: An earth sign of the Zodiac, April 20–May 20, symbolized by a bull.

Underworld: In many cultures, the land of the dead, ruled by a very powerful god or goddess.

Undines: One of the elemental creatures representing water.

Virgo: An earth sign of the Zodiac, August 23–September 22, represented by a young woman.

Waning Moon: In the cycle of the moon, the time after the Full Moon and before the New Moon. Practitioners of magic use this time to create spells to reduce things.

Waxing Moon: In the cycle of the moon, the time after the New Moon and before the Full Moon. Practitioners of magic use this time to create spells to increase things.

West: One of the directions called by neo-pagans and Wiccans. The West is symbolized by water. The West is represented by sunset, swimming creatures, and bodies of waters including the ocean, ponds, and rivers.

Wheel of the Year: The neo-pagan term for the eight holidays of the years. The quarter days are the two equinoxes and two solstices. The cross-quarter days are Imbolc, Beltane, Lammas, and Samhain.

Wicca: The neo-pagan religion celebrating the Divine as Goddess and God. Centered around a celebration of nature and practiced ethically by the Rede: 'an it harm none, do what thou wilt.

Widdershins: In neo-pagan and Wiccan ritual practice, moving backward around the circle. The circle is created deosil or clockwise, to uncreate or open the circle celebrants move left.

Yemaya: African goddess of the ocean.

Yule: The winter solstice celebration, December 21.

Zephyrus: Greek God of the West Wind.

Zeus: Greek god, King of the Gods.

Zodiac: The set of constellations that tracks the journey of the sun, symbolizing the year.

Works Consulted

Bloch, Douglas and Demetra George. *Tarot for Yourself: A Workbook for Personal Transformation*. Oakland: Wingbow Press, 1989.

Goodman, Linda. *Linda Goodman's Sun Signs*. New York: Bantam, 1968.

Greene, Liz. *Mythic Astrology*. New York: Simon and Schuster, 1994.

Lewis, C. S. *The Magician's Nephew*. New York: Macmillan, 1955.

Meltzer, Brad. *The Tenth Justice*. New York: Warner Books, 1998.

Nietzsche, Friedrich. *The Complete Works of Friedrich Nietzsche*. Stanford: Stanford University Press, 1999.

Sams, Jamie and David Carson. *Medicine Cards: The Discovery of Power Through the Ways of Animals*. New York: St. Martin's Press, 1999.

Starhawk. *Dreaming the Dark: Magic, Sex and Politics*. Boston: Beacon Press, 1997.

———. *Spiral Dance: A Rebirth of the Ancient Religion of the Goddess*. San Francisco: HarperSanFrancisco, 1999.

————. *Truth or Dare: Encounters with Power, Mystery and Authority*. San Francisco: HarperSanFrancisco, 1999.

Thorsten, Geraldine. *The Goddess in Your Stars: The Original Feminine Meaning of the Sun Signs*. New York: Simon and Schuster, 1989.

White, E. B. *Charlotte's Web*. New York: HarperCollins, 1997.

We'Moon Calendar 00. Estacada, Ore.: Mother Tongue Ink, 1999.

Reading in the Dark

A Booklist

Adler, Margot. *Drawing Down the Moon: Witches, Druids, Goddess-Worshipers and Other Pagans in America Today.* Boston: Beacon Press, 1986. Revised and expanded edition.

Begg, Ean. *The Cult of the Black Virgin.* London: Arkana, 1986.

Breuton, Diana. *Many Moons: The Myth and Magic, Fact and Fantasy of Our Nearest Heavenly Body.* New York: Prentice-Hall, 1991.

Budapest, Zsusanna E. *Grandmother Moon: Lunar Magic in Our Lives: Spells, Rituals, Goddesses, Legends, and Emotions Under the Moon.* San Francisco: HarperSanFrancisco, 1990.

Cabot, Laurie and Tom Cowan. *Power of the Witch: The Earth, the Moon and the Magical Path to Enlightenment.* New York: Delta, 1989.

Conway, D. J. *Moon Magic: Myth & Magic, Crafts & Recipes, Rituals & Spells.* St. Paul: Llewellyn, 1995.

Eason, Cassandra. *Moon Divination for Today's Woman.* London: Foulsham, 1994.

Eclipse. *The Moon in Hand: A Mystical Passage*. Portland, Maine: Astarte Shell Co., 1991.

Fox, Matthew. *Original Blessing*. Santa Fe: Bear & Co., 1983.

Galland, China. *Longing for Darkness: Tara and the Black Madonna*. New York: Viking, 1990.

George, Demetra. *Finding our Way Through the Dark: The Astrology of the Dark Goddess Mysteries*. San Diego: ACS Publications, 1995.

————. *Mysteries of the Dark Moon: The Healing Power of the Dark Goddess*. San Francisco: HarperSanFrancisco, 1992.

Glass-Koentop, Pattalee. *Year of Moons, Season of Trees: Mysteries and Rites of Celtic Tree Magic*. St. Paul: Llewellyn, 1991.

Grimassi, Raven. *The Wiccan Mysteries: Ancient Origins & Teachings*. St. Paul: Llewellyn, 1998.

Hall, Nor. *The Moon and the Virgin: Reflections on the Archetypal Feminine*. New York: Harper and Row, 1978.

Kryder, Rowena Pattee. *The Faces of the Moon Mother: An Archetypal Cycle*. Mount Shasta, Calif.: Golden Point Publications, 1991.

McCoy, Edain. *Lady of the Night: A Handbook of Moon Magic & Rituals*. St. Paul: Llewellyn, 1995.

Meador, Betty DeShong. *Uncursing the Dark: Treasures from the Underworld*. Willmet, Ill.: Chiron Publications, 1992.

Mountainwater, Shekhinah. *Ariadne's Thread: A Workbook of Goddess Magic*. Freedom, Calif.: The Crossing Press, 1991.

Perera, Sylvia Brinton. *Descent to the Goddess: A Way of Initiation for Women*. Toronto: Inner City Books, 1981.

Reis, Patricia. *Through the Goddess: A Woman's Way of Healing*. New York: Crossroad Publishing Co., 1991.

Rush, Anne Kent. *Moon, Moon*. New York: Random House, 1976.

Starhawk. *Dreaming the Dark; Magic, Sex & Politics*. Boston: Beacon Press, 1984.

Starck, Marcia and Gynne Stern. *The Dark Goddess: Dancing with the Shadow*. Freedom, Calif.: The Crossing Press, 1993.

Woodman, Marion and Elinor Dickson. *Dancing in the Flames: The Dark Goddess in the Transformation of Consciousness*. Boston: Shambhala, 1996.

Zweig, Connie and Jeremiah Abrams. *Meeting the Shadow: The Hidden Power of the Dark Side of Human Nature*. Los Angeles: Jeremy P. Tarcher, 1991.

Zweig, Connie and Steve Wolf. *Romancing the Shadow: Illuminating the Dark Side of the Soul*. New York: Ballantine, 1997.

Index

☾ REACH FOR THE MOON

Llewellyn publishes hundreds of books on your favorite subjects! To get these exciting books, including the ones on the following pages, check your local bookstore or order them directly from Llewellyn.

Order by Phone
- Call toll-free within the U.S. and Canada, 1-800-THE MOON
- In Minnesota, call (651) 291-1970
- We accept VISA, MasterCard, and American Express

Order by Mail
- Send the full price of your order (MN residents add 7% sales tax) in U.S. funds, plus postage & handling to:

  Llewellyn Worldwide
  P.O. Box 64383, Dept. 0-7387-0095-9
  St. Paul, MN 55164–0383, U.S.A.

Postage & Handling
- **Standard** (U.S., Mexico, & Canada)

If your order is:

$20.00 or under, add $5.00

$20.01–$100.00, add $6.00

Over $100, shipping is free

(Continental U.S. orders ship UPS. AK, HI, PR, & P.O. Boxes ship USPS 1st class. Mex. & Can. ship PMB.)

- **Second Day Air** (Continental U.S. only): $10.00 for one book + $1.00 per each additional book
- **Express** (AK, HI, & PR only) [Not available for P.O. Box delivery. For street address delivery only.]: $15.00 for one book + $1.00 per each additional book
- **International Surface Mail:** Add $1.00 per item
- **International Airmail:** Books—Add the retail price of each item; Non-book items—Add $5.00 per item

Please allow 4–6 weeks for delivery on all orders.
Postage and handling rates subject to change.

Discounts
We offer a 20% discount to group leaders or agents. You must order a minimum of 5 copies of the same book to get our special quantity price.

Free Catalog
Get a free copy of our color catalog, *New Worlds of Mind and Spirit*. Subscribe for just $10.00 in the United ed States and Canada ($30.00 overseas, airmail). Many bookstores carry *New Worlds*—ask for it!

Visit our website at www.llewellyn.com for more information.

BOOK OF HOURS
Prayers to the Goddess

Galen Gillotte

*Poetic, mystical, lyrical
Goddess-centered prayers*

Here is a book that moves beyond the conscious mind and into the heart and spirit. It is not about theory, techniques of ritual, or even of "practice."

It is, simply, a book of goddess-centered prayers, meditations, and affirmations. It includes morning, evening, and nightly prayers; seasonal prayers (for the Wiccan holy days); and prayers for the new and full moons.

Essentially, prayer is speaking with Deity, but many people are confused about how to do this. This book will alleviate the confusion. It is written for young and old, for the neophyte as well as the accomplished Priest or Priestess. It may be used in Wiccan circles, study groups, or anytime you want to connect to the Goddess. Ultimately, it is for those who have a deep hunger for that spiritual connection.

1-56718-273-9, 168 pp., 5³⁄₁₆ x 8, hardcover $14.95

CELESTIAL GODDESSES

An Illustrated Meditation Guide

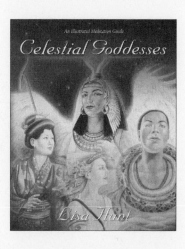

Lisa Hunt

Original art in this volume depicts twenty goddesses in all their heavenly beauty. These goddesses personify the heavens, and gave birth to the sun, the moon, and the stars. They had the power to create and to restore lives. Now you, too, can nurture and celebrate the feminine divine with the help of *Celestial Goddesses*.

Visualize your own spiritual journey with the aid of twenty original, full-color goddess paintings. From Amaterasu (Japan), whose brother's jealous rampage helped her realize her true beauty, to the creation myth of Mawu (West Africa), each image is accompanied by a description of the symbolism and a guided meditation. Hardcover with full-color interior.

- Goddesses representing twenty different cultures will appeal to readers from various backgrounds

- Each goddess has a poignant story that invites you to relate to her in a very personal way

- A wonderful addition to New Age, fantasy, astrology, and astronomy book collections; this book can be used on many different levels: as an art collection, as an overview of ancient celestial goddess worship, and as a meditative guide

0-7387-0118-1, 144 pp., 8 x 10,
full-color interior, hardcover $24.95

CELTIC WOMEN'S SPIRITUALITY

Accessing the Cauldron of Life

Edain McCoy

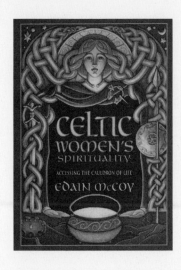

Every year, more and more women turn away from orthodox religions, searching for an image of the divine that is more like themselves—feminine, strong, and compelling. Likewise, each year the ranks of the Pagan religions swell, with a great many of these newcomers attracted to Celtic traditions.

The Celts provide some of the strongest, most archetypally accessible images of strong women onto which you can focus your spiritual impulses. Warriors and queens, mothers and crones, sovereigns and shapeshifters, all have important lessons to teach us about ourselves and the universe.

This book shows how you can successfully create a personalized pathway linking two important aspects of the self—the feminine and the hereditary (or adopted) Celtic—and as a result become a whole, powerful woman, awake to the new realities previously untapped by your subconscious mind.

1-56718-672-6, 352 pp., 7 x 10, illus.   **$16.95**

WOMEN CELEBRATING LIFE

A Guide to Growth & Transformation

Elizabeth Owens

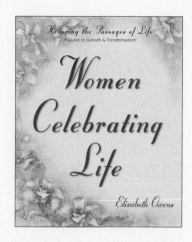

Whether you're turning 21 or 50, having a baby or entering menopause, you can embrace and honor the events in your life through meaningful rituals. In solitude, you can perform ceremonies that will release pent-up emotions, soothe old wounds, and nurture the feminine spirit.

This book is a how-to manual written to help women manifest a more fulfilling existence. It gives specifics on how to perform ceremonies to raise a woman's consciousness, attract happy circumstances, and promote healing of the emotions. In an age where society sings the praises of the young, *Women Celebrating Life* recognizes and cheers the spiritual attributes of women who have experienced life.

1-56718-508-8, 216 pp., 7½ x 9⅛   **$12.95**

TO ORDER, CALL: 1-800 THE MOON
Prices subject to change without notice.

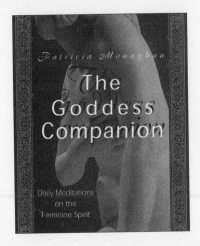

GODDESS COMPANION

Daily Meditations on the Feminine Spirit

Patricia Monaghan

Engage your feminine spirit each day of the year! Here are hundreds of authentic goddess prayers, invocations, chants, and songs—one for each day of the year. They come from dozens of sources, ranging from the great classical European authors Ovid and Horace, to the marvelously passionate Hindu poets Ramprasad and Ramakrishna, to the anonymous gifted poets who first composed the folksongs of Lithuania, West Africa, and Alaska. In fresh, contemporary language that maintains the spirit of the originals, these prayers can be used for personal meditation, for private or public ritual, or for your own creative inspiration. They capture the depth of feeling, the philosophical complexity, and the ecological awareness of goddess cultures the world over.

Organized as a daily meditation book, *Goddess Companion* is also indexed by culture, goddess, and subject, so you can easily find prayers for specific purposes. Following each prayer is a thoughtfully written piece of prose by Patricia Monaghan that illustrates the aspects of the Goddess working in our everyday lives. There is a perpetual calendar with a daily reading on each page.

Includes prayers from Greece, Rome, North and South America, Lithuania, Latvia, Japan, Finland, Scandinavia, India, and many others, in translations that fully reveal their beauty, making them immediately accessible and emotionally powerful

1-56718-463-4, 312 pp., 7½ x 9⅛   **$17.95**

GODDESS MEDITATIONS

Barbara Ardinger, Ph.D.

Bring the presence of the Goddess into your daily spiritual practice with *Goddess Meditations*, a book of seventy-three unique guided meditations created for women and men who want to find a place of centeredness and serenity in their lives, both alone and in groups, either in rituals or informally.

Call on a Hestia for a house blessing . . . the White Buffalo Calf Woman for help in learning from your mistakes . . . Aphrodite for love and pleasure . . . Kuan Yin for compassion. Although it's directed toward experienced meditators, this book includes guidelines for beginners about breathing, safety, and grounding, as well as instructions for rituals and constructing an altar.

Also featured is the powerful "Goddess Pillar Meditation," based on the Qabalistic Middle Pillar Meditation; nine Great Goddess meditations that address issues such as protection, community, and priestess power; and seven meditations that link goddesses to the chakras.

1-56718-034-5, 256 pp., 7 x 10   **$17.95**

THE GODDESS PATH

Myths, Invocations & Rituals

Patricia Monaghan

For some, the goddess is a private intellectual search, where they can speculate on her meaning in culture and myth. For others, she is an emotional concept, a way of understanding the varying voices of the emerging self. Then there are those for whom she is part of everyday ritual, honored in meditation and prayer. All are on the goddess path.

If you have never encountered the goddess outside your own heart, this book will introduce you to some of her manifestations. If you have long been on this path, it will provide prayers and rituals to stimulate your celebrations. *The Goddess Path* offers a creative approach to worship, one in which you can develop and ritualize your own distinctive connection to her many manifestations from around the world.

Includes invocations, myths, symbols, feasts, and suggestions for invoking the following goddesses: Amaterasu/Self-Reflection; Aphrodite/Passion; Artemis/Protection; Athena/Strength; Brigid/Survival; Cailleach/Power in Age; Demeter & Persephone/Initiation; Gaia/Abundance; Hathor/Affection; Hera/Dignity; Inanna/Inner Strength; Isis/Restorative Love; Kali/Freedom; Kuan-Yin/Mercy; The Maenads/Ecstasy; The Muses/Inspiration; Oshun/Healing; Paivatar/Release; Pomona/Joy; Saule & Saules Meita/Family Healing.

1-56718-467-7, 288 pp., 7½ x 9⅛, illus.   **$14.95**

GREEN WITCHCRAFT II

Balancing Light & Shadow

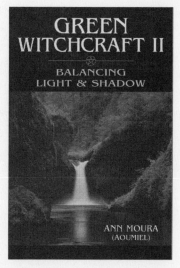

Ann Moura

The Green Witch is a natural witch, a cottage witch, and a solitary witch. This witch does not fear nature and the woods, but finds a sense of belonging and connection with the earth and the universe. Now, in this sequel to *Green Witchcraft*, hereditary witch Ann Moura dispels the common misunderstandings and prejudices against the "shadow side" of nature, the self, and the Divine. She presents a practical guide on how to access and utilize the dark powers in conjunction with the light to achieve a balanced magical practice and move towards spiritual wholeness.

Guided meditations, step-by-step rituals, and spells enable you to connect with the dark powers, invoke their energies, and achieve your goals through magical workings. Face your greatest fears so you can release them, create an elemental bottle to attract faery life, burn herbs to open your subconscious awareness, learn to use the ogham for travel to other worlds, recognize and name a familiar, and much more.

1-56718-689-0, 288 pp., 6 x 9   **$12.95**

INVOKE THE GODDESS

Visualizations of Hindu, Greek & Egyptian Deities

Kala Trobe

Appeal to the Hindu goddess Sarasvati to help you ace an exam. Find your ideal long-term partner through Isis. Invoke Artemis for strength and confidence in athletics or fitness.

Invoke the Goddess shows you how to link with the specific archetypal energies of fifteen different goddess through simple exercises and visualizations. This magickal workbook allows anyone, no matter how limited or developed her occult prowess, into a direct encounter with a powerful archetypal deity whose symbols and presence will make a profound impression on the subconscious.

Whether you want to accomplish a specific goal or integrate the murkier areas of your psyche, this book will lead you step by step through your inner journeys. The author explains different ways of carrying out the exercises, how to take ritual baths with solarized water, and preparation through chakra work, diet, and exercise.

1-56718-431-6, 240 pp., 7½ x 9⅛, illus.   **$14.95**

IN PRAISE OF THE CRONE

A Celebration of Feminine Maturity

Dorothy Morrison

When Dorothy Morrison began her menopausal metamorphosis at the early age of 32, she thought her life was over. Then she discovered a reason to celebrate: she'd been invited to the Crone's party!

Meet your hostess and mentor, your Personal Crone. Mingle a bit and find your Spirit Self. Discover why the three of you belong together. Learn to balance yourself, gather wisdom, reclaim your life, and make the most of your natural beauty. Then meander into the Crone's kitchen and find home remedies that can take the edge off minor menopausal aggravations without the use of hormone replacement therapy or prescription drugs.

Written with humor and compassion from someone who's been there, *In Praise of the Crone* alleviates the negativity and fear surrounding menopause with a wealth of meditations, invocations, rituals, spells, chants, songs, recipes, and other tips that will help you successfully face your own emotional and spiritual challenges.

1-56718-468-5, 288 pp., 6 x 9 **$14.95**

MAGICK & RITUALS OF THE MOON

Formerly titled *Lady of the Night*

Edain McCoy

Harness the energy of "Lady Luna"

Moon-centered ritual, a deeply woven thread in Pagan culture, is often confined to celebration of the full moon. Edain McCoy revitalizes the full potential of the lunar mysteries in this exclusive guide for Pagans.

Magick & Rituals of the Moon explores the lore, rituals, and unique magickal potential associated with all phases of the moon: full, waxing, waning, moonrise/moonset and dark/new. Combined with an in-depth look at moon magick and rituals, this book offers a complete system for riding the tides of lunar magick.

Written for both solitary and group practice, *Magick & Rituals of the Moon* breaks new ground by showing how both men and women can Draw Down the Moon for enhanced spirituality. Pagans will find fun and spirited suggestions on how to make the mystery of the moon accessible to non-Pagans through creative party planning and popular folklore.

0-7387-0092-4, 256 pp., 7 x 10   **$14.95**

MAIDEN, MOTHER, CRONE

The Myth and Reality of the Triple Goddess

D. J. Conway

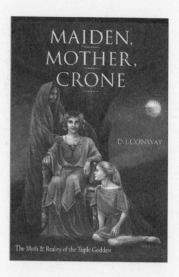

The Triple Goddess is with every one of us each day of our lives. In our inner journeys toward spiritual evolution, each woman and man goes through the stages of Maiden (infant to puberty), Mother (adult and parent), and Crone (aging elder). *Maiden, Mother, Crone* is a guide to the myths and interpretations of the Great Goddess archetype and her three faces, so that we may better understand and more peacefully accept the cycle of birth and death.

Learning to interpret the symbolic language of the myths is important to spiritual growth, for the symbols are part of the map that guides each of us to the Divine Center. Through learning the true meaning of the ancient symbols, through facing the cycles of life, and by following the meditations and simple rituals provided in this book, women and men alike can translate these ancient teachings into personal revelations.

Not all goddesses can be conveniently divided into the clear aspects of *Maiden, Mother and Crone*. This book covers these as well, including the Fates, the Muses, Valkyries, and others.

0-87542-171-7, 240 pp., 6 x 9   **$12.95**

THE NEW BOOK OF GODDESSES AND HEROINES

Patricia Monaghan

They come out in your dreams, your creativity, your passion, and in all of your relationships. They represent you in all your glory and complexity, and you represent them. They are the goddesses and heroines that form our true history. Your history. Let these mythic stories nourish your soul as they speak to you on a level as deep and mysterious as the source of life itself.

The third edition of this classic reference offers a complete, shining collection of goddess myths from around the globe. Discover more than 1,500 goddesses in Australia, Africa, North and South America, Asia, Europe—and experience her as she truly is. This new edition also adds hundreds of new entries to the original text—information found only in rare or limited editions and obscure sources.

There is a new section on "Cultures of the Goddess," which provides the location, time, and general features of the major religious system detailed in the myths. A comprehensive index, titled "Names of the Goddess," provides all available names, with variants. Stories, rites, invocations, and prayers are recorded in the "Myths" section, as well as a list of common symbols. Never before has such a vast panorama of female divinity been recorded in one source.

1-56718-465-0, 384 pp., 8½ x 11, illus., photos $19.95